Julia Maria Colton

**Annals of Switzerland**

Julia Maria Colton

**Annals of Switzerland**

ISBN/EAN: 9783337152321

Printed in Europe, USA, Canada, Australia, Japan

Cover: Foto ©Andreas Hilbeck / pixelio.de

More available books at **www.hansebooks.com**

# ANNALS

OF

# SWITZERLAND

BY

JULIA M. COLTON

NEW YORK
A. S. BARNES AND COMPANY
LONDON: HODDER & STOUGHTON
1897

TO

## A. L. P.

"Ah, Fredome is a noble thing ;
Fredome makes man to haiff lyking :
Fredome all solace to man giffis,
He levys at ease that freely levys."

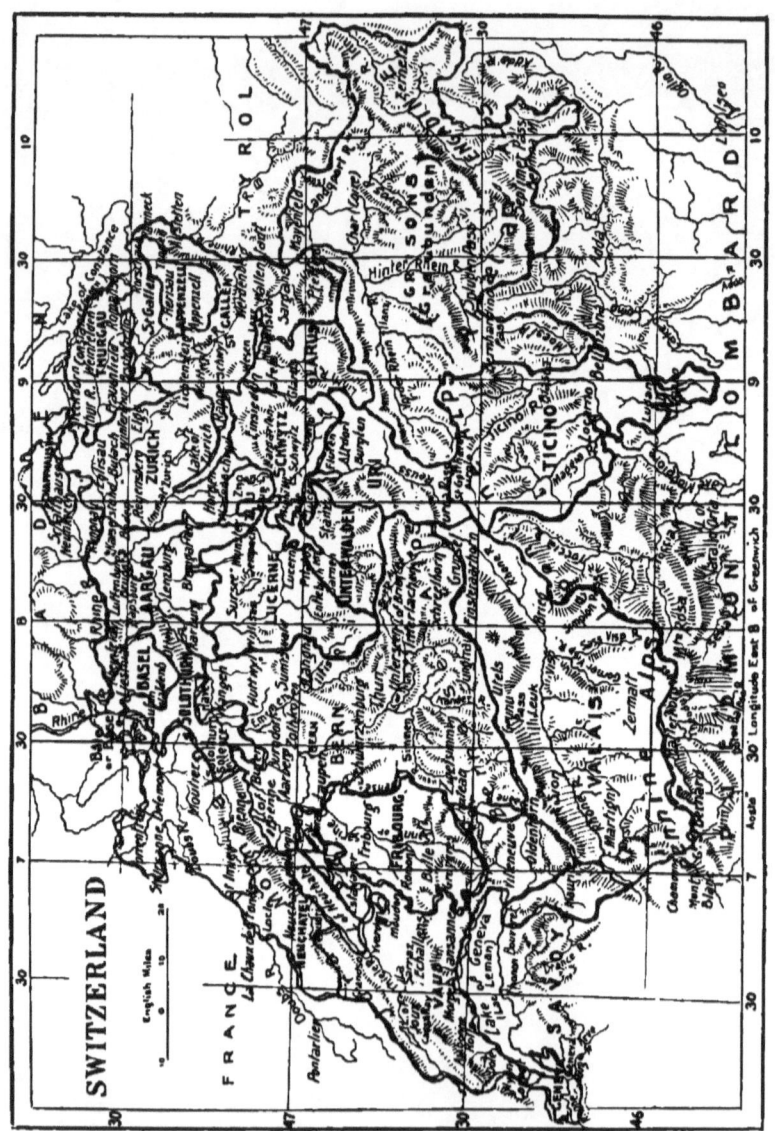

# PREFACE

IT seems strange that Switzerland, a country so popular among tourists, so extolled by every lover of nature, so appreciated by those who realize
"What pleasure lies in height!"
should have found few to chronicle in the English tongue the inspiring events of her history. Many records have been written in the native German and French languages, but for the English reader, the fragmentary facts of the guide-book have provided the chief historical information concerning a land where the blood-red of the battle-field is environed with prismatic tints of romance.

It is the aim of the "Annals of Switzerland" to present a brief, consecutive narrative of the struggles, progress, and attainments of a race of freemen; but traditions which belong as truly to the land as do its glaciers and avalanches cannot be ignored in pages which seek to depict the development of this democracy, founded three centuries before the Reformation.

J. M. C.

BROOKLYN, May 6, 1897.

# CONTENTS.

| CHAPTER | | PAGE |
|---|---|---|
| I. | Helvetia | 5 |
| II. | Supremacy of the Franks, Imperial Rule, and Zeringen Dynasty | 13 |
| III. | The League of Three Lands | 21 |
| IV. | Growth of the Confederacy | 37 |
| V. | The Era of Sempach and Näfels | 51 |
| VI. | The Council of Constance | 64 |
| VII. | Civil Wars and the Everlasting Compact | 74 |
| VIII. | War with Burgundy | 85 |
| IX. | Grandson, Morat, and Nancy | 95 |
| X. | League of Thirteen Districts | 112 |
| XI. | Mercenary Service and the French Alliance | 123 |
| XII. | The Apostle of Switzerland | 131 |
| XIII. | The Religious Struggle | 141 |
| XIV. | Geneva | 153 |
| XV. | Conflicts and Controversies | 170 |
| XVI. | The Victory Won | 180 |
| XVII. | Calvin in Geneva | 192 |
| XVIII. | The Borromean League | 204 |

## Contents.

| CHAPTER | | PAGE |
|---|---|---|
| XIX. | Freedom from the Empire | 214 |
| XX. | Progress in Political Enfranchisement | 226 |
| XXI. | The Era of the French Revolution | 237 |
| XXII. | The League of Rothen | 252 |
| XXIII. | The Sonderbund War | 271 |
| XXIV. | The Constitutions of 1848 and 1874 | 281 |

# LIST OF ILLUSTRATIONS.

| | | |
|---|---|---|
| Cantonal Coats of Arms | | *Frontispiece.* |
| Map of Switzerland | | *facing p.* vii |
| Chamonix: Le Groupe de De Saussure et le Mont-Blanc | " | 5 |
| Brunnen | " | 19 |
| Tell's Chapel | " | 31 |
| Altdorf: Statue of William Tell | " | 35 |
| Luzern | " | 37 |
| Lake of Thunn | " | 57 |
| Martigny: The Castle | " | 71 |
| Bluebeard's Castle, near Interlaken | " | 81 |
| The Jungfrau | " | 91 |
| Map of Burgundy | " | 95 |
| Clock Tower at Bern | " | 119 |
| Lauterbrunnen | " | 127 |
| Seal of Zurich | " | 140 |
| Zurich | " | 145 |
| Castle of Chillon | " | 161 |
| The Reformers | " | 173 |
| Lake of Geneva | " | 187 |
| Cathedral of St. Peter, Geneva | " | 195 |
| St. Gothard Pass | " | 209 |

## List of Illustrations

| | | |
|---|---|---|
| Wesen | *facing p.* | 221 |
| Maloja | " | 227 |
| Lion of Luzern | " | 237 |
| Goeschennen | " | 261 |
| Near Klosters — Silbretta Glacier | " | 275 |
| The Axenstrasse | " | 285 |

# AUTHORITIES.

| | |
|---|---|
| Daguet | Abrégé de l'Histoire Suisse. |
| Zschokke | History of Switzerland. |
| Duruy | History of France. |
| Hallam | History of Middle Ages. |
| Kirk | History of Charles the Bold. |
| Coxe | House of Austria. |
| D'Aubigné | History of Reformation. |
| Fisher | History of Reformation. |
| Seebohm | History of Reformation. |
| Bryce | Holy Roman Empire. |
| Christoffel | Life of Zwingli. |
| Grote | Letters on Switzerland. |
| Winchester | Swiss Republic. |
| Adams & Cunningham | Swiss Confederation. |
| Bernard Moses | Federal Government of Switzerland. |

CHAMONIX : LE GROUPE DE DE SAUSSURE ET LE MONT-BLANC.

# ANNALS OF SWITZERLAND

## CHAPTER I

### HELVETIA

BORNE upon wavering wings of tradition, a legend floated long ago over the Alps, to begin the story of Switzerland. Falling to earth in the region near the sources of the Rhine and the Inn, the legend told of a people from Italy, — perhaps kindred to the Etruscans, — who, wandering northward during years veiled amid myths, rested where the district of Rhetia preserved the name of the tribe, as well as that of their god Rhetus.

Neither revelatory legend, nor archæological research has traced the ties of kinship between the Rhetians and the Latin race of Lake-dwellers, whose architectural and domestic remains have procured their introduction to the modern world, but both claim recognition among ancestors of the Swiss. Wanderers from Scandinavia, under the guidance of the brothers Switer and

Swen, are reputed to have founded the Canton of Schwyz; and the Grecian emigrants from Massilia, whose journey to the Lake of the remote Wilderness[1] was chronicled by Herodotus, have also been named among predecessors of the Helvetic nation.

In the region bounded by the Rhine, the Jura mountains, Lake Leman, and the Lake of Constance, authentic history begins four or five centuries before the Christian era, when the land was occupied by a valorous people, living in separate communities. Each community was independent within its own district, unless a common interest rendered union of strength advantageous, as in the case of peoples on the Rhine and the Thor, whose compact gave to their united lands the surviving name of Thurgau.

*The Helvetians.*

We find records of warlike expeditions among the tribes occupying this territory during the last years of the second century B. C., when a martial impulse had been excited by the exploits of their neighbors, the Cimbri and Teutones, and in search of both glory and spoil forces of their strong men were sent to join the "confederates from many nations" in an invasion of Gaul. The Gauls, thus menaced, sought

---
[1] Lake Leman.

Roman aid; a Roman army was directed to march toward the homes of the men of Thurgau, who, suddenly recalled from pursuit of plunder, hastened under a valorous young leader, named Diviko, to encounter the Roman legions.  On the banks of Lake Leman,[1] Diviko achieved a brilliant victory; the Romans lost their commander — the consul Lucius Cassius — were forced to sue for quarter, and, after passing disarmed under the yoke erected for their humiliation by command of the conqueror, they were sent over the mountains with the story of their disgrace.

*Contact with Rome.*

The victorious Diviko then returned to Gaul, and, uniting his forces with those of the Cimbri, passed into Italy; but Rome summoned her Consul Marius out of Africa, and in the battles of Aix and Vercellæ (102–101 B. C.) the barbarian hosts suffered such overwhelming defeats that the survivors from their ranks sought hasty refuge amid the mountains.  The fugitives settled in a district afterwards divided into the four cantons of Uri, Schwyz, Unterwalden, and Luzern, where, in conjunction with occupants of the neighboring valleys, they were

*Diviko.*

---

[1] Most historians name the shores of Lake Leman as the theatre of this battle, but Mommsen, and a few other authorities place it on the borders of the Garonne, near Santons.

known as Helvetians, a people mentioned by Cæsar as inhabitants of twelve towns and four hundred villages.

The glory gained at Lake Leman, and glowing reports from the adjacent pasture-lands of Gaul, sufficed to stimulate again the ambition of this stalwart people, and Hordrich, or Orgetorix, an influential man among them, proposed that the entire community should emigrate and seek possessions in that more fruitful district. The project was received with a degree of favor Project of Orgetorix. that insured immediate preparations for its execution, — preparations continued until the leader's zeal had well-nigh wrecked the enterprise. To consummate friendly compacts with princes of Gaul, Orgetorix bound his daughter by a marriage contract with one of the number; but the prospective alliance aroused suspicion that personal aggrandizement was the principal aim of the Helvetian, and he was immediately summoned before a popular tribunal, to answer this accusation. Orgetorix responded by defiantly arming his retainers, whereupon the entire community denounced him as a traitor and demanded his death by fire. To escape this fate the chief committed suicide.

This tragic episode did not divert the Helvetians from the pursuit of their purpose; and, after three years spent in preparation for the emigration, they burned their houses to preclude all thought of a return, and carrying provisions for three months went forth under the guidance of the aged Diviko.  With their allies from neighboring lands they were computed to number three hundred and sixty-eight thousand, of whom ninety-two thousand were warriors.

*Emigration and Subjugation.*

This exodus occurred in the year 60 B. C., and Cæsar was then in Gaul.  He first encountered the Helvetians near Geneva, where an attack upon the rear-guard of their army resulted in victory for the trained legions of Rome; but, instead of seeking an immediate engagement with the entire force of invaders, Cæsar, while strengthening his own army, allowed the enemy to advance, until on the borders of the Saône he was able to strike so effective a blow that the surviving remnant of the Helvetian host were powerless to resist the decree which ordained their immediate return to their desolated land.  Cæsar annexed their territory to Gallia Celtica, and granted to the humbled people the title of Roman allies; but he erected on Lake Leman the new fortress of Noviodunum (Nyon), in order, from that point, as from other strongholds, soon scattered along their frontiers, to keep the tribes of Helvetia under the Argus eye of Rome.

Heedless of the subjugation of their neighbors, the sturdy folk in Rhetia, with allies along the borders of the Inn, and in the valleys of the Tyrol, pursued their custom of plundering travellers across their borders, and, secure in the retreats afforded by their mountain passes, often descended into Italy for purposes of pillage. In the reign of Augustus these incursions grew formidable, and legions under the successive commands of Drusus and Tiberius were sent against the intruders. After an obstinate struggle the Rhetians were subdued; their district, with the mountain lands east, was included in the empire under the name of Rhetian, Norican, and Pannonian provinces, and permanent Roman garrisons were established to secure the subjection of the people.

*The Rhetians.*

Although thus under imperial control, the peasants were permitted to retain their simple laws; and, in an assembly of deputies from the combined districts, they chose their own magistrates, and decided questions of common interest. Under the immediate successors of Augustus, the inhabitants of Helvetia paid taxes and served in the Roman armies, as good and loyal subjects of the em-

*The Roman Sway.*

pire, while Aventicum, their seat of government, became a magnificent city with institutions similar to those in Italian towns of the period.

In the year 70 A. D. the emperor Galba was assassinated in Rome, and in the provinces Roman officials speedily formed leagues for the election of his successor. Before the people of Helvetia had heard of Galba's death, Aulus Cecina, their governor, sent messengers throughout every district to command allegiance to Vitellius. Believing that they were loyal to their emperor in their act, the Helvetians intercepted the messengers, and armed to oppose the governor. Cecina marched against them with a large force, sacked Baden, then one of their principal cities, and having defeated the insurgents in battle, sold many into slavery, and commanded the immediate execution of Julius Alpinus, the chief man in the community.[1]

With the tidings of their defeat, the Helve-

---

[1] Fifteen hundred years afterwards this inscription is said to have been discovered in the ruins of Aventicum: "I lie here; Julia Alpinula; unfortunate child of an unfortunate father. Priestess of the goddess Aventia, my prayers failed to avert the death of my father; fate had decreed that he should die ignominiously. I lived to the age of twenty-three."

Although, through the criticism of Lord Mahon, this alleged memorial has been denominated a forgery of the seventeenth century, Byron accords the priestess a credulous note of sympathetic admiration.

tians first heard of the death of Galba, and ambassadors were immediately dispatched to implore pardon for an unintentional opposition to legitimate authority. But the arrogant soldiers who had raised Vitellius to the throne, demanded the total extirpation of the race of peasants whose loyalty had opposed their will; and, although the eloquent pleading of the Helvetian envoy obtained a mitigation of the penalty and rescued the lives of the offenders, the punishment ordained terminated their history as a nation. Their country was incorporated with the province of Gaul, and the distinctive name of Helvetia was legally ignored. Gradually Roman customs were introduced, the Latin language encroached to some extent upon the ancient speech, and, under the mild dominion of Nerva, Trajan, Hadrian, and the Antonines, the people, turning from warlike pursuits to the cultivation of their land, again achieved prosperity.

# CHAPTER II

### SUPREMACY OF THE FRANKS, IMPERIAL RULE AND ZERINGEN DYNASTY

#### A. D. 200–1200.

During the closing years of the Roman supremacy, and through several succeeding decades, the region north of the Alps lay open to occupation by the nomadic tribes who were pushing their way toward Italy, and much obscurity rests upon its annals. From a confusing record of conflicts which indicate frequent interchange of realm among the migrating nations, we emerge in the year 500, when the southwestern portion of the country now called Switzerland belonged to the Burgundians, the northern territory was shared between the Franks and the Allemanni, and Rhetia was claimed by the Ostrogoths. The distinction between the languages spoken in Switzerland has been traced to this period, when the people in the dominions of the Allemanni spoke a Gothic tongue, and those under Burgundian rule a Gallo-Roman dialect, from which was developed the Provençal, to be followed by the modern French.

In the latter part of the fifth century, during an inroad upon Gallic territory, the Allemanni met the army of Clovis, King of the Franks, and suffered a defeat which implied subjection; and during the sixth century, by the dissolution of the old Burgundian kingdom and the fall of the empire of the Ostrogoths, the remaining districts, formerly occupied by the three nationalities, were transferred to the kingdom of the Franks.

<small>Divisions under Clovis.</small>

The new sovereign divided the land according to the languages spoken therein. One division was joined to Swabia, while another, under the name of Little Burgundy, became a part of Savoy. The population included the conquered inhabitants, ingrafted colonies from Rome, and remnants of the various Teutonic tribes who had in succession occupied the districts. The subjugated people became serfs of the Gallic lords, and, although occasionally allowed a voice in matters of legislation, they were denied the privilege of bearing arms.

<small>Introduction of Christianity.</small> Varied legends ascribe the entrance of Christianity among them to Beatus, in the first century; to Lucius, a Rhetian,

in the third; and at the close of the fourth century to members of the Theban Legion. Gallus, a disciple of St. Columbanus, had, previous to that period, established his hermitage near the Lake of Constance, where stands to-day the sadly-modernized convent of St. Gall; and Meinrod had built his cell, lived in poverty, and died a violent death on the spot marked by the stately Abbey of Einsiedeln, which legendary lore designates as having been consecrated by angels. As early as 843 was founded there the "record-chamber," the nucleus of a noted library. Religious institutions multiplied under the sovereignty of the Franks, and whoever was baptized, had learned a prayer, and could make the sign of the cross, was called a Christian, even though heathen customs and superstitions continued to dominate his life.

Laws were few in an age that regarded protection of property for the individual as the ultimate object of jurisdiction, and when theft was regarded as a greater crime than murder. A form of trial by jury was occasionally practised, but judgment was more frequently rendered through the medium of the ordeal.

Knowledge of letters was an almost exclusive endowment of the clergy, who, through this instrumentality, were enabled to acquire wide political as well as spiritual influence. The monastery of St. Gall became noted as a centre of learning where medieval culture attained its zenith, while its temporal prosperity was attested by the possession of one hundred and sixty thousand acres of land.

With Charlemagne's sovereignty a new era dawned, for under his liberal patronage many institutions for popular instruction were founded. To his bounty, symbolized as a "fountain of intellectual life," Zurich attributes her first schools, and other cities included within the boundaries of Switzerland ascribe their early literary impulses to the stimulating influence of the first sovereign of the "Holy Roman Empire."

*Charlemagne.*

In the division of Charlemagne's empire, the Helvetian territory was tossed like a ball from hand to hand, until caught in the grasp of the newly-organized German monarchy. Counts and seignors in the land from thenceforth paid feudal allegiance to the Emperor, but in his own domain each was allowed absolute control of "the soil, with man, beast, and tree." Upon these vast feudal estates, in addition to the customary tribute of fowls and eggs, rendered to the seignor, each householder was assessed for an annual tax of a tenth of his crops or other wealth, and upon the death of the father of a family his children yielded up whatever had been his most valued possession, — beast, garment, or furniture.

The seignors in adjacent districts were usually at feud with one another, unless some common danger threatened, when individual jealousies were temporarily controlled, and forces were joined for mutual protection.

Gradually the inhabitants of the open country gathered in villages, for which a religious house or a baronial mansion served as a nucleus. Each village enjoyed a special jurisdiction under its *vogt* or bailiff; but at a general assembly, held in the open air, all important questions were settled, and any person who possessed "seven feet of land before or behind him" might claim a voice in this council. *Growth of Cities.*

In the tenth century, when Magyar hordes, from the north and east, swept with barbaric fury through Germany, the Emperor Henry I. commanded that the larger villages should be walled, that, thus protected, they might serve as places of refuge for peasants of the neighboring country. In the unsettled state of the empire, the population of villages thus fortified rapidly increased, and when an imperial decree conferred special privileges upon all their residents who were not bondsmen, a thrifty burgher class[1] arose, and prospered.

The name of a city often records some distinctive characteristic of its early days, as Schaffhausen on the Rhine, which originated in a cluster of boathouses, or *Schiffhäusern*, and Luzern, where the old *Lucerna*, or light-house (now called the *Wasserthurm*), indicates the origin of the city.

Freemen of noble birth who possessed small landed estates were chosen members of the councils in these villages, and, proud of a position of authority in the "Holy Roman Empire," they assumed the name of "patrician," — a title retained until the close of the middle ages.

In the eleventh century, when contests between the Emperor Henry IV. and Pope Gregory VII. had called forth the bull of excommunication that freed all imperial subjects from their oaths of allegiance, a Diet held at Forschew deposed Henry and declared Rudolf of Swabia Emperor of Germany; Henry returning from his enforced pilgrimage to Rome, found himself crownless, and Rudolf in possession of sovereign power. In the war that

---

[1] Residents of a *burg*, or fortress.

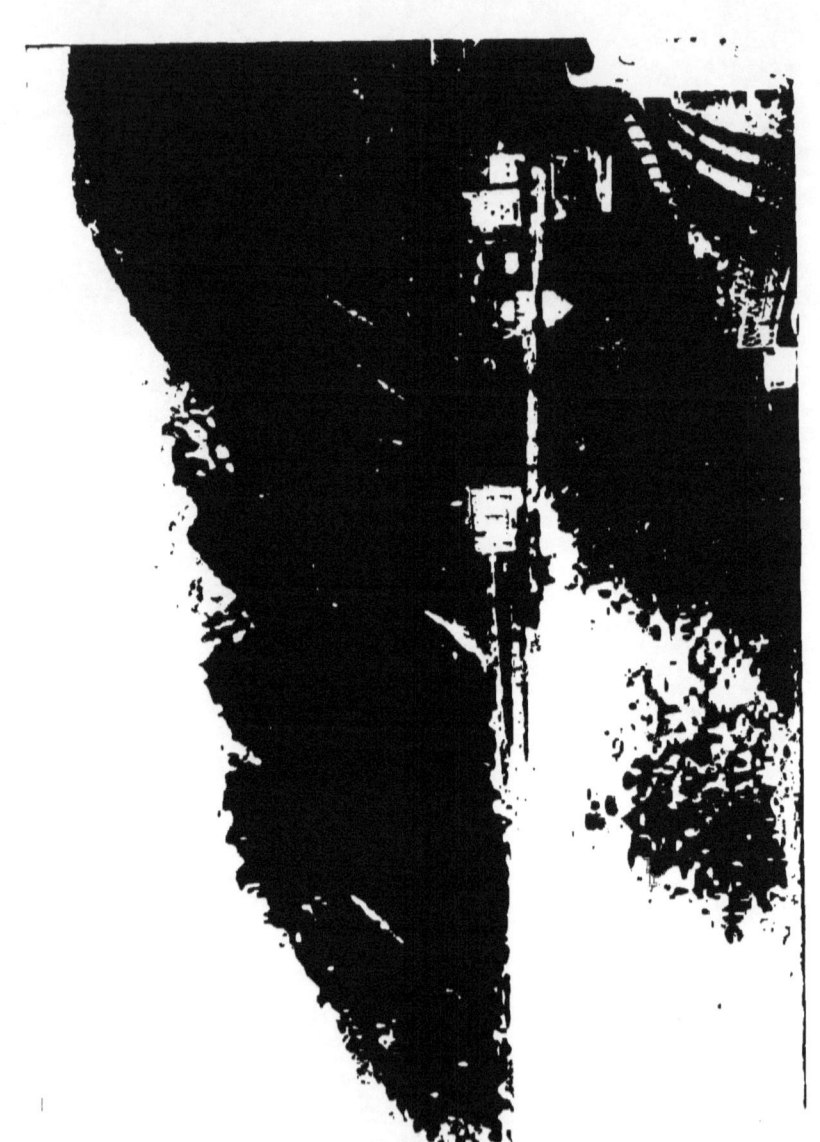

BRUNNEN.

ensued, although the Pope sent a consecrated crown to Rudolf, fortune declared in favor of Henry; Rudolf was slain in the battle of Merseburg, by the hand of Godfrey de Bouillon, and his Swabian dukedom was bestowed upon Frederick of Hohenstaufen, son-in-law of Henry IV. Rudolf's son, however, continued the war until his death, ten years later, when his claims were transferred to his brother-in-law Berchthold II. of Zeringen. A compromise was then effected, by which the greater portion of the Helvetian territory was given to Berchthold, as a fief of the empire, and, during several generations, dukes of his family, known as the "thirty lords of Zeringen," retained the sovereignty.

It was during the period of Zeringen rule that the name of the free men of Schwyz came for the first time into prominence. **The Free Men of Schwyz.** In a sheltered district upon Lake Luzern dwelt these descendants of the Helvetians, who had continued to exercise, unmolested, all the privileges of a free community throughout the stormy years in which their land had been passed from sovereign to sovereign. Although they recognized the Emperor of Germany as their feudal superior, these peasants had remained unrestricted in their choice of the Ammann who presided over their local courts of justice, and had acknowledged no foreign obligation beyond the payment of imperial tribute-money.

Ignorant of the fact that Henry II. had donated large tracts of land, adjacent to their own, for the enrichment of monasteries, or as rewards to seignors, these shepherds of Schwyz came into unforeseen conflict with the Abbot of Einsiedeln, whose flocks were feeding upon their mountains. The Abbot claimed as much as he chose of the uninclosed territory, and appealed for support to the head of the empire, whose decision in favor of the ecclesiastic apprised the inhabitants of the valley that their allegiance was no guarantee of protection. Rejecting, thenceforth, all obligations imposed by imperial mandate, they declared, "We have no need of an emperor if he cannot secure our rights," and having cemented a defensive alliance with their neighbors of Uri and Unterwalden, they defied the imperial authority. Despite anathemas and decrees from Emperor and from Pope, the attitude of hostility toward Einsiedeln was maintained; priests were compelled to conduct religious services, though papal sanction was denied, and during an age of universal servitude the brave peasants of Schwyz preserved a prosperous independence.

# CHAPTER III

## THE LEAGUE OF THREE LANDS

### 1200-1315.

AFTER the extinction of the house of Zeringen, the entire territory, formerly subject to their control, was ruled by the counts and seignors whose castles clung to the mountain sides or dotted the level country. According to Watteville, there were in the thirteenth century no less than fifty counts, one hundred and fifty barons, and one thousand noble families within the confines of modern Switzerland. Prominent among these petty sovereigns were three ecclesiastical princes, — the Bishop of Chur, the Abbot of St. Gall, and the Abbess of Säckingen, — and the Counts of Kyburg, Rapperswyl and Hapsburg in the list of temporal lords. The last-named nobles owned only a small territory west of the Steinen, but Count Albert III. secured the office of vogtship or imperial bailiff over a larger district than any member of his family had previously controlled, and his son Rudolf obtained the advocacy of a region embracing the three districts of Uri, Schwyz, and Unterwalden. His duties in this office included those of the president of criminal tribunals, arbitrator in civil dissensions, guardian of the highway, and representative of the people at the imperial court.

In 1217 the intervention of the advocate Rudolf I. secured a temporary cessation of the prolonged hostilities between Schwyz and Einsiedeln; but when Rudolf II. claimed hereditary authority to govern the district, and attempted to restrict the liberty of the peasants, the three valley-communities sought imperial sanction in their defence of privileges exercised by their ancestors. In response to the appeal from Uri, a formal release from Hapsburg **Rule of Hapsburg Lords.** over-lordship was granted in 1231, with a special charter of franchises, and in 1240 a document, addressed "to all the inhabitants in the valley of Swites," gave that district also deliverance from the jurisdiction of the counts of Hapsburg, and immunity from all but imperial taxation. But the domineering knight who continued to claim the authority of an advocate in the territory practically ignored the imperial charters, and compelled obedience to his arbitrary decree from the peasants of

## The League of Three Lands 23

Schwyz and Uri, as well as in Unterwalden, where he possessed estates. In protestation against this bondage, the men of the three districts in 1245 concluded, by a verbal compact, their first defensive league.

As a means of establishing his authority on the shores of Lake Luzern, Rudolf erected there a castle; but this was destroyed five years later, and for half a century no fortress walls marred the Arcadian landscape. During the contests between Frederick II. and Innocent IV. the Hapsburgers sided with the Pope, and the men of the forest cantons took the part of the Emperor; but in the decline of Frederick's authority, the Hapsburgs, like other nobles of the empire, found opportunity for their own aggrandizement, and in 1273 Count Rudolf III. was elected Emperor of Germany.

For a score of years the imperial crown had been loosely controlled by various factions, who, by turns, bestowed it upon one foreign candidate or another, until, weary of the existing confusion, yet jealous of their own authority, the electors sought a man strong enough to punish criminals, with whom the country was flooded, yet weak enough to need for every mandate the sanction of the

*Rudolf III. of Hapsburg*

princes. Their desires were bluntly defined by the Bishop of Olmutz, who wrote to the Pope: "They wish to obtain, through the grace of the Holy Ghost, a gracious emperor, — through the wisdom of the Son of God, a wise emperor; but they ignore the first person in the Trinity, and power is their abhorrence."

Rudolf's rival for the imperial honors was Ottacar of Bohemia, a war with whom, following the election, resulted in the acquisition by the Hapsburgs of Styria, Carniola, and Carinthia. These provinces Rudolf bestowed upon his two sons, whereupon Albert, the elder son, assumed the title of "Duke of Austria." Rudolf's elevation is said to have been largely due to the influence of Werner, Archbishop of Mentz, who had received favors at the hands of the Count of Hapsburg, for which he promised recompense. In order to insure the necessary votes for Rudolf, the Archbishop hinted to the electors, who were chiefly unmarried men, that his candidate had six marriageable daughters; whereupon the election was immediate and unanimous.

But the Count of Hapsburg had not so favorably impressed all ecclesiastics, for the Bishop of Basle is reported to have exclaimed, when he heard of the election, "Lord God!

set thyself fast upon thy throne, else surely this Rudolf will pluck thee down from it."

Rudolf's imperial administration of eighteen years, popular and widely equitable, induced a confiding submission to legitimate authority. But although the Emperor recognized the charter of Uri, he refused to confirm the privileges claimed by Schwyz, and two weeks after his death the men of that community joined the patriots of Uri and Unterwalden in a "Perpetual Alliance" for mutual aid in resisting oppressions. August 1, 1291, deputies from the three districts signed the *Bundesbrief*, which embodied in written form the terms of the verbal contract of 1245. *[The Perpetual Alliance or "Bundesbrief."]*

This Latin *Bundesbrief*, still preserved in the archives of Schwyz, records the formal inauguration of the oldest free state in the world. With the motto "All for one, and each for all," it united the members of the league against any "who should use violence toward them, or cause injury to one or to all." While recognizing the duty of allegiance to the Emperor, the communities declared a resolution to preserve their prerogatives in matters of legislation, and in case dissensions should arise, they claimed perfect freedom in the choice of arbitrators.

Upon the death of the Emperor Rudolf, his son Albert assumed the imperial crown, without awaiting the action of a diet; but received proof of his unpopularity when Adolf of Nassau was chosen head of the empire. The new sovereign possessed little influence among princes, but he confirmed the imperial franchises of Uri and Schwyz, and the three forest districts (Waldstätten) embraced his cause. Thereupon Albert, conciliating some of the electors, kindled a partisan war, in which Adolf was defeated and slain; Albert, succeeding to his authority, refused to recognize the franchises claimed by the Waldstätten, and by imperious and unscrupulous acts thoroughly alienated the people. Although there is no authentic record of a direct attack upon the liberties of the land, yet a host of legends, bearing reference to tyrannical aggressions, have centred around the period, and mingle so indissolubly with the history of the age that they demand narration.

According to these stories, Albert sent an Austrian official to exercise authority in the districts of the Waldstätten, and when the allied peasants claimed the right to demand in his place an imperial bailiff, Hermann Gesler, and Berengen of Landenberg, contrary to all former usages, took up their abode in the land. Gesler built a fortress, which he called "Uri's Restraint," while Landenberg located himself with equal security in Unterwalden, and both by arbitrary and tyrannical rule violated the franchises, and exasperated the people. The taxes were increased, the smallest offence severely punished, and the peasants continually insulted.

In Landenberg's district of Unterwalden lived Arnold of Melchthal, whose punishment for some trifling offence was the confiscation of his oxen. The official sent to seize them jeeringly said, "If peasants wish for bread they may draw the plough themselves." Stung by this insult, Arnold offered resistance, and broke the fingers of one of the men. He then fled to the mountains to escape the bailiff's vengeance; but Landenberg caused the arrest of his aged father, whose eyes were put out in expiation of the son's offence. "That puncture," says an old chronicler, "went so deep into many a heart that numbers resolved to die rather than leave it unrequited."

In the village of Steinen, the freeman Werner Stauffacher built a house whose comfort aroused the jealousy of Gesler, and the bailiff's comment, "Shall a vile peasant build himself a house without permission from his lord?" was quoted throughout the region. Urged onward by his heroic wife, Stauffacher joined Arnold of Melchthal and Walther Fürst of Uri in a solemn oath to free the land from its tyrants; and in the meadow of Rütli, on the shore of Lake Luzern, the three men held midnight consultations, when each brought assurances from the persecuted communities they represented, that death was more desirable than bondage. On the night of November 11, 1307, each leader guided to the trysting-place ten trusted men, to whom their heroic purposes were revealed; and at sunrise, raising their hands to heaven, all joined in an oath which consecrated them to the service of freedom. Then, appointing New Year's night, 1308, for the accomplishment of their enterprise, they returned to their homes.

Meanwhile, Gesler, suspicious of the fidelity of the people in his district, had ordered a pole to be erected in the village of Altorf, upon which the ducal cap of Austria was fastened, that homage to this symbol of authority might be publicly rendered. For disregard of this decree, *William Tell.* William Tell, the son-in-law of Walther Fürst, and one of the oath-bound men of Rütli, was seized and carried before the bailiff. His reputation as a marksman was widespread, and, making his skill the instrument of punishment, Gesler commanded him to shoot an apple from the head of his son. The amazing deed was successfully accomplished; but a second arrow in the archer's quiver aroused inquiry, and upon receiving a promise of pardon, Tell incautiously revealed his resolution to shoot Gesler had his son been the first victim. The terrified bailiff, declaring that his promise secured the life but not the freedom of the marksman, commanded the immediate arrest of Tell, who, securely bound, was placed in the boat awaiting Gesler's return to his castle at Küssnacht. Half-way across the lake a storm arose, the boat became unmanageable by the boatmen, and the prisoner, known to be a superior seaman, was unbound, and ordered to take the helm. Steering the craft toward a rocky shelf of land that protruded at the base of the Axenberg, Tell suddenly seized his bow, and sprang ashore, while the boat, rebounding, carried Gesler and his men far out upon the lake. They succeeded in landing when the storm had abated; but Tell meanwhile had sought a hiding-place, from whence, as the bailiff passed, was sent forth a well-aimed arrow, that pierced the tyrant's heart.

So runs the tale, and with it belongs the legend, current in Switzerland, that Tell and the three men of Rütli are asleep in the mountains, but will awake to the rescue of their land should tyranny ever again enchain it.[1]

The ancient chroniclers proceed to relate that at midnight on New Year's eve, 1308, a *Capture of Landenberg's Castle.* girl in Landenberg's castle threw a rope to her lover, waiting below her window, and by this device twenty of the

---

[1] Although the pitiless criticism of modern historical work has forced the exploits of Tell into the domain of the mythical, yet a degree of credence is given to the story that may render interesting a summary of evidence in favor of its truth.

As early as 1307 a religious service is claimed to have been instituted in Switzerland to commemorate the deed of the hero, and in the following year a chapel was erected on the spot where he was reputed to have landed from Gesler's boat. This chapel was dedicated in the presence of one hundred and twenty-four persons said to have known Tell personally. The history of the marksman is given in the chronicle of Klingenberg that bears record through the fourteenth century; in an ancient "Ballad of Tell" preserved in the archives of Sarnen; in the "Chronicle of Russ" which bears the date of 1482; and in the "Chronicle of Eglof" of the fifteenth century. His deeds are recorded by Tschudi in 1570, and allusion is made to them as historical by other early writers. At the end of the sixteenth century doubts of the authenticity of the stories were first circulated, and in 1760 the book of a Bernese named Freudenberger, was publicly burned in Uri, for denial of the historical accuracy of current accounts of Tell's life. But other works were soon written to spread the awakened incredulity; and Voltaire contributed to the scepticism by his comment, "Ces histoires des pommes sont toujours suspectes."

TELL'S CHAPEL.

oath-bound men of Rütli were secretly drawn within the walls of Rotzberg. In the early morning twenty of their confederates, who came with customary gifts to the bailiff, were invited within the gates, when, drawing out concealed pikeheads, they fixed them upon their staves, and sounded a call that brought reinforcements from neighboring hiding-places. Almost without resistance, the stronghold of the tyrant was captured; but Landenberg and his men were suffered to go free upon taking an oath to quit the country forever. The spirit of liberty was now fully aroused; Gesler's "Restraint" and other fortresses were demolished, and the people in the three districts bound themselves by the oath of Rütli.

. . . . . . . .

Under Albert's direction was compiled "The Terrier," a kind of Doomsday Book for the Austrian provinces. It enumerated the estates of the Hapsburgers, and recorded the quit-rents, dues, etc., for which the tenants were liable. The inventory for a similar record was begun in Switzerland, but was interrupted by the death of the Emperor, who, while returning from a conference at Baden, was assassinated by his nephew, John of Swabia. On the banks of

<small>"The Terrier."</small>

<small>Assassination of Albert.</small>

the Reuss, at Windisch, Albert became accidentally separated from his suite, and John found his opportunity for revenge upon the relative who had defrauded him of his paternal estates. By the aid of Walter of Eschenbach and Rudolf of Balm,[1] the fatal assault was made, and the royal victim was left to die in the arms of a peasant woman.

The assassins soon realized that they had been deceived in the expectation of support after this bloody deed, and safety was sought by flight, while the terrified land offered no resistance to the vengeance of the Emperor's adherents, who, believing that a formidable league existed, punished all suspected of complicity. Castles were burned to the ground, and a thousand victims perished. Agnes, the daughter of Albert, is said to have witnessed the executions, and her exclamation, "Now I bathe in May dew!" interprets the spirit with which the house of Austria pursued the unfortunate confederates through many succeeding years.

On the accession of the new emperor, Henry of Luxemburg, the freemen of Schwyz opposed the work of the officials charged with the survey of their land for "The Terrier," and Henry confirmed to Schwyz and Uri the franchises

---

[1] *Ulric* de Baum is the name given by some historians.

covered by their earlier charters, and granted to Unterwalden all privileges enjoyed under his predecessors. But failing thus to keep a promise to the Hapsburgers for the recognition of their claims in the districts, he incited the dukes of Austria to efforts for the maintenance of prerogatives which they regarded as hereditary.

In 1313 Henry of Luxemburg died, and Frederick, the eldest son of Albert of Austria, opposed Louis of Bavaria as candidate for imperial honors; Frederick, being the first to secure recognition, determined to regain the inheritance of his family in the three valley districts; and when an attack made by the men of Schwyz upon the domains of their ancient enemy, the Abbot of Einsiedeln, afforded a pretence for interference, he charged his brother, the gloomy Leopold of Austria, with the execution of the project. *Contests with Imperial Rulers.*

In 1315, prepared "to tread the boors under foot," and carrying with him wagonloads of cordage, wherewith to hang the ringleaders among the confederates, Leopold proceeded to Baden, where he held a council of war. A triple attack was concerted. The main force, fifteen or twenty thousand strong, was ordered to advance from Zug *1315.*

under Leopold himself, while Count Otho of Strassburg, with four thousand men, was to march over the Brünig, and one thousand troops from Luzern, crossing the lake, would join the others at Unterwalden.

Confident of victory, the Duke's division advanced in stalwart battalions, their leader the ideal of chivalry. The confederates, concluding hasty terms of alliance with Glarus, Urseren, and Interlaken, scornfully rejected the offered terms of peace, stationed themselves by command of Rudolf Reding on a ridge of the Sattel, offered their prayers, and awaited the enemy. At early dawn, on the 15th of November, the narrow defile of Morgarten, where the ascent into the uplands of Schwyz begins, was crowded with Austrian troops. Tradition relates that fifty men of Schwyz, who had returned from banishment on this eventful day, but were denied admittance into the ranks of their countrymen, ascended another ridge of the mountain, and hurled down rocks upon the advancing hosts. Into the confusion thus created rushed the confederate bands, striking down with their heavy clubs Austrian knight and soldier, many of whom were trodden to death by their own cavalry. There was no room for retreat except in the universal flight

*Battle of Morgarten.*

ALTDORF : STATUE OF WILLIAM TELL.

which ensued after an hour and a half of desperate strife. The invading army left the flower of their nobility upon the field, and Leopold, escaping with difficulty, reached Winterthur, says the chronicle, "pale and in despair."

The following morning, confederate troops marched to meet the men from Luzern, who had landed at Bürgenstadt, and easily forced them to retreat to their ships. The victors then turned toward a third detachment of the enemy, who had advanced across the Brünig, but who, learning of the defeat of their associates, hastily retreated. In a chapel dedicated to St. Jacob, on the confines of the canton of Zug, the Swiss erected a memorial of their victory, and here, on the anniversary of "the glorious battle of Morgarten," a commemorative service is annually held. A few weeks after the battle (Dec. 9, 1315), deputies from the Waldstätten met at Brunnen,[1] and concluded a new treaty of alliance, by which obedience to the seignors of the districts was still yielded, unless it should conflict with duty toward the confederacy, loyalty to which was forever to dominate all other claims.

<small>The Brunnen "Bund."</small>

---

[1] At Brunnen is this inscription: "Hier wurde der ewige Bund geschworen, Anno 1315, die Grundfeste der Schwyz."

The confederates appealed to Louis IV. for the removal of the ban launched against them by Frederick, and an imperial decree annulled all prerogatives of the house of Hapsburg in the Waldstätten. Involved in wars for the compensating possession of the imperial throne, the Duke of Austria made peace with the confederates, in 1318, renouncing all claims in their territory except over hereditary estates of the Hapsburgs; and the three communities, treating with Austria on equal terms, covenanted to enter no alliance antagonistic to their ancient enemy. This treaty, annually renewed, preserved peace until the year 1323.

LUZERN.

# CHAPTER IV

**GROWTH OF THE CONFEDERACY**

1332–1376

THE protective strength of the three valley-communities, in an age of general oppression, tempted neighboring towns to seek admission to their league, and entrance was first granted to Luzern. The burghers of that city had enjoyed many franchises under the mild government of Murbach Abbey, until financial embarrassments had compelled the sale, to Rudolf of Hapsburg, of certain rights of feudal jurisdiction over the territory. When the Duke by an increase of taxes, forcible enlistment of troops, and other acts of arbitrary despotism, rendered his authority oppressive, Luzern was stimulated to throw off the recently-imposed yoke, and, as a preliminary step, concluded with the Waldstätten a treaty for twenty years.

 *Luzern.*

Upon learning of this alliance, the Hapsburg nobility in Aargau declared war, in the name of

Austria, while within Luzern the aristocratic families united in a conspiracy for opening the gates to the enemy's forces. A legend tells how a boy who chanced to overhear their plans was discovered by the conspirators and made prisoner, but, regarded as too young to betray them, he was released after having taken an oath to reveal the secret to no man. Passing from the custody of his captors into a hall where some burghers were assembled, the boy related his story in a loud voice to the stove, easily attracting the attention of the citizens, who, through this timely warning, were able to arrest the leaders in the plot. Before sunrise of the following day the giant peaks of Pilatus and Rigi, which shadow the ancient city, were watch-towers for a free people. The government of Luzern was taken from the families who had controlled it under the Duke of Austria, and was vested in a council of three hundred burghers.

*1332.*

Zurich next joined the confederacy. That city, the Roman "Turicum," endowed by the early Carlovingians with privileges that insured its rapid growth, had become eminent both for commercial and intellectual activity. Its minster, enlarged and enriched by Charlemagne, dates backward to

*Zurich.*

the period of the introduction of Christianity by the Theban legion. The oldest Christian legend of the country tells how two members of the Theban band, Felix and Regula, refused to sacrifice to the gods, and were condemned to death by the Romans. After prolonged sufferings the martyrs were executed, but picking up their severed heads, they walked with them to the summit of a hill in the vicinity of Zurich, and buried themselves there in a spot now consecrated to the patron saints of the city. In 853, Louis the German donated extensive lands to the convent of Felix and Regula, of which his daughter Hildegarde was abbess, and the district was granted exemption from all jurisdiction save that of the king.

The Emperor, Frederick II., made Zurich a free city, and in the thirteenth century it became a centre of intellectual life, where minnesingers and scholars received liberal patronage. During the interregnum new privileges were acquired, which were confirmed by Albert of Austria. The government was vested in the hands of a council elected by the citizens, but official caprice obtained frequent opportunity for indulgence through the wide liberty of action allowed in unforeseen circumstances. Complaints of oppression were rife, when a member of the council, named Rudolf Brun, being at variance with his own party, instigated the citizens to demand an account of the public moneys. The council delayed action, regarding the manifested discontent as only a transient mood of the populace; but the impression that their deputies had been trifled with spread among the burghers, the council chamber was besieged, and the members with difficulty effected an escape. Brun was then appointed burgomaster for life, and a new constitution gave the artisans of the town a voice in its government.

But exiled members of the old council meditated vengeance, and plotted at Rapperswyl to regain possession of the city through a midnight massacre. Again the legends tell of a listening apprentice and a convenient stove. From behind that familiar household mechanism, which would seem to merit immortal honor in Switzerland, the boy overheard schemes which, when reported to Rudolf Brun, caused him to don his armor in hot haste; while alarm bells summoned the citizens to arms, and men, women, and children joined in pursuit of the retreating enemy. Few of the conspirators escaped punishment, and Count John of Rapperswyl, for his support of their cause, suffered the devastation of his lands, while even adjacent Austrian territory was ravaged, in the frenzy for retaliation that ensued. Fearing the revenge of the Duke, Zurich then sought alliance with the Waldstätten, and in 1351 became fifth member of the confederation. The city differed from other allies in the reservation of a right to form private alliances, provided the terms made were subordinate to those of the confederate bond.

Although the conflict with Austria was continued, succeeding years were marked by increased strength in the confederacy, through the admission of new members. Glarus, a dependency of the monastery of Säckingen, over which the Hapsburgers claimed the authority of advocates, had been summoned to aid Austria in the execution of vengeance upon Zurich and the Waldstätten; but, animated by sympathy with the conduct of the confederates, the burghers of Glarus refused obedience to the Duke, and despatched two hundred of their young men to the assistance of the threatened city. Joining the army of the Waldstätten, this company aided in defeating an Austrian army on the field of Rütli; and soon after that event Glarus was admitted into the confederacy, though upon a footing somewhat inferior to the other members.

*Glarus.*

In Zug, a district lying between Zurich and the Waldstätten, a majority of the population

**Zug.** were in sympathy with the confederates, but the town remained faithful to Austria until threatened by the victorious Zurichers. Then the Duke's indifference to her danger gave excuse for the admission of the confederate army, and in 1352 Zug was sheltered within the *Bund*.

Bern, founded in 1191 by Berchthold V. of Zeringen, to signalize his exploit in killing

**Bern.** a bear upon the spot,[1] had rapidly attained a position of prominence, and boasted an early charter, distinguished by its seal of beaten gold. Made a free city of the empire by Frederick II., the sovereignty of Bern was swiftly extended over a wide circuit which embraced many growing towns. The strength thus acquired aroused the jealousy of noble families in the vicinity, but on the Dornbuhl, and at Oberwangen, the burghers were victorious over the combined forces of their antagonists, and at the close of the thirteenth century Bern became the most influential city in the district now covered by the Swiss confederation. But neighboring

---

[1] "From a monster slain, let there be a name to the future city."

seignors maintained a hostile attitude, and continued their efforts to force from the city council a recognition of Austrian authority, until, failing in every attempt at conciliation, the burghers of Bern prepared to assert their independence in the face of the invading foe. The projects of their enemies had been sanctioned by the Emperor, and "seven hundred barons with crowned helmets, twelve hundred knights, and eighteen hundred soldiers" formed the force that drove the terrified peasants into the city, where leading men in the enemy's camp, with confident anticipation of victory, had already selected their mansions. The town of Laupen, in the canton of Bern, was first threatened, and six hundred men from the city of Bern, with nine hundred allies from the Waldstätten, were sent to its relief, under command of Rudolf of Erlach.[1]

While the leaders of the hostile bands were occupied in exchanging messages of defiance, Diebold of Basilwind, a Teutonic knight, and a priest of Bern, promised heavenly rewards to all who should meet death in their defence of liberty. The conflict between the two powerful armies was prolonged and fierce, but the stout burghers of Bern at length gained the

[1] Some historians name John of Bubenberg as commander.

mastery, and their routed enemy fled, leaving fifteen hundred from their ranks upon the field. Then, after a night passed upon the battle-ground, according to their custom, the exultant Bernese marched homewards, bearing the captured banners of twenty-seven noble families. The victory at Laupen gave freedom to Bern, for, although hostilities were prolonged during several years, the domination of the nobility was ended.

At the termination of the conflict Erlach relinquished the authority with which he had been temporarily invested, and retired to his castle of Reichenbach, where a few years later he met a tragic death. In 1353 Bern entered into full covenant with Uri, Schwyz, and Unterwalden, making the eighth member of the league, which for more than a century received no additional support. The three original allies were under mutual obligations, while those who had more recently joined the *Bund* were in alliance with the Waldstätten, but, unless bound by a special private covenant,[1] remained independent of one another. Zurich was made *Vorort* or directing canton,

---

[1] Luzern was thus allied with Zurich and Zug; Zurich with Luzern, Zug, and Glarus; Glarus with Zurich only; Zug with Luzern and Zurich; Bern with only the original trio.

and upon her territory, in the open-air assemblies, called *Landesgemeinden*, the burghers, summoned by a loud bell, gathered annually on the last Sunday in April to deliberate upon all matters of common interest, either in peace or war. After the celebration of a religious service, the business of the day consisted of an inspection of the annual accounts, the promulgation of new laws, and the election of new officials. Free discussion was permitted, and a vote of assent was signified by the elevation of the hand. The final ceremony was the installation of the *Landammann*, or chief magistrate, who was required to take an oath of fidelity to the terms of the *Bundesbrief*, and to exchange with the people oaths of loyalty.

<small>Zurich Vorort.</small>

<small>Landesgemeinden.</small>

In the predatory warfare that still existed between members of the league and Austria, the troops of the Duke had suffered repeated defeats, and Albert, anxious to terminate the contest, sought to collect an army that should finally overpower the "obstinate peasants" who defied his authority. In 1352, a force of thirty thousand foot and four thousand horse were intrusted to Everhard, Count of Würtemberg, who immediately laid siege to Zurich. The city, although unprepared for the attack, defended itself until the besieging army were fellow-sufferers in a bitter famine, and Albert was glad to accept the terms of an agreement known as the "Brandenburg peace." In this compromise, revenues from Schwyz, Unterwalden, and Luzern were guaranteed the Duke; and Glarus and Zug, though preserving their connection with the Helvetic league, were again placed under the domination of Austria. But disputes relative to the interpretation of special terms of this treaty soon arose, and Albert appealed to the Emperor as umpire. Charles VI., allied by family ties to the house of Hapsburg, displayed so strong a partiality for the interests of the Duke, that the Swiss promptly declined to accept his mediation, and, irritated by this rejection of his authority, the Emperor refused to recognize their confederacy.

*The Brandenburg Peace.*

With the declaration, "members of the empire can form no compact without the imperial consent," Charles despatched an army to join that of the Duke, again encamped before Zurich; but Albert, disheartened by repeated reverses, soon abandoned his plan of operations, and forbade the name of the Swiss to be mentioned in his presence. The imperial forces were also soon recalled, and a

*Peace of Ratisbon.*

peace, concluded at Ratisbon in 1355, terminated the fruitless contest.

* * * * * *

The great plague that desolated so large a portion of Europe and Asia in the fourteenth century was disastrous to Switzerland, where estates were left without claimants and towns were depopulated. *Great Plague. Flagellants.* The Jews, suspected of having originated the scourge by poisoning the wells, suffered everywhere terrible persecutions; and when these measures produced no diminution in the death-roll, religious fanaticism was awakened, and fraternities known as Flagellants wandered through the land, doing penance for the sins of the world. They bore a letter reputed to have been written in marble by the Divine hand, which announced that God had determined upon the immediate destruction of the world, but mercy would be shown those who, acknowledging their sin, should unite in deeds of penitence. Commands of Pope and princes forbidding the extravagant practices of the sect, were alike defied, but as the virulence of the disease abated, their influence declined. At the end of four years, although excitement had thoroughly disorganized the afflicted districts, and eradicated the civilizing work of generations; yet, in the words of an old chronicler, "The world began again to be merry, and men made them new clothes, and sang new songs."

In 1370, the Waldstätten, with Zurich and Zug, adopted the *Pfaffenbrief*, or "Letters of the Priests," a strong protest against the abuse of power by the clergy. This document, one of great importance in the development of Swiss government, is remarkable for having introduced the principle of the authority of a majority in the adoption of new statutes. As a result of the tenets it embodied, nobles in want of pecuniary resources prompted the towns to tax ecclesiastics, and the emboldened peasantry refused to render to their priests many former services of vassalage. But with the decline of clerical authority, the power of the nobility also waned, and many of that class, who had rivalled the house of Austria in tyrannical rule, prepared a way for the overthrow of their own authority in giving sanction to the *Pfaffenbrief*.

<small>The Pfaffenbrief.</small>

At this period neither sovereign nor city maintained a standing army,[1] but feudal obligations compelled the enrolment for military

---

[1] Charles the Bold of Burgundy was the first prince to discern the advantages to be derived from the maintenance of a standing army.

## Growth of the Confederacy 49

service of noble, burgher, and peasant, at the summons of prince, seignor, or city council. When this obligation became burdensome, or less absolute, as the feudal system declined, bands of penniless men were assembled, willing to undertake any enterprise for money, who, ranging over the Continent, proffered mercenary service. Such bands were originally gathered in Italy, where the soldiers received the name of *condottieri*. <small>The Condottieri.</small>

Arnold of Cervola, an Italian captain out of employment, undertook a predatory excursion into Switzerland, and advanced against Basle, where the fortifications had recently been weakened by an earthquake. The inhabitants of the city begged aid of the confederates, and fifteen hundred troops were despatched to defend this important outpost, whereupon Cervola retreated without venturing an attack. Ten years later Ingram de Courcy, son-in-law of Edward III. of England, declared a feud against Austria, on the ground of the non-payment of dowry promised his mother, the daughter of Duke Leopold I. The reigning Duke, Leopold III., pretended that the dowry lands had fallen into the possession of the Swiss, and summoned them to aid against De Courcy. The Waldstätten declared that sacrifice of troops for the protection of a hostile power was impossible, but promised to remain neutral, while Bern and Zurich, whose territory was exposed to attack, sent forces to join the army of Austria. On the approach of the invaders a panic seized both the Austrian troops and their Swiss allies; and fleeing before encountering the enemy, they abandoned to De Courcy's plundering bands the entire country from the Jura to the gates of Bern. This aroused the Waldstätten, and for self-protection they despatched a band of men from Luzern and Unterwalden to join the troops from Entlibuch. The combined forces encountered and defeated De Courcy's men, near Büttisholz (1376), where a mound, still called the "English barrow" (*Engländer Hügel*), remains as a prominent monument of the battle.

*Battle of Büttisholz.*

## CHAPTER V

### THE ERA OF SEMPACH AND NÄFELS

#### 1376–1412

A SLIGHT anachronism may be detected in the picture representing the burghers of Solothurn standing upon the walls of their city to witness the creation of Adam and Eve; but an inscription upon its cathedral ascribes to the town a veritable antiquity that in north-western Europe is antedated by Trèves alone.

*Solothurn.*

A knight of the fourteenth century, Count Rudolf of Kyburg, cherished the belief that he possessed by inheritance a claim upon Solothurn, and, failing to establish his title through the authority of archives, he plotted a secret seizure of the ancient city. Aided by the prior of the cathedral, with whom he claimed kinship, and by the canon, John Amstein, who lived upon the city walls, the Count arranged for the secret admission of his armed retainers.

On the appointed night, in darkness and in silence, the foe advanced; but, unseen by them, a peasant named John Rott, who had learned their traitorous projects, ran forward and warned of impending danger the watchman at the eastern gate. Attempting to sound the city bells, the watchman found them muffled; but cries of alarm echoing through the streets aroused the inhabitants, and when the Count of Kyburg reached the walls he found them guarded by armed and resolute men, from whose presence he hastily retired.

The treacherous canon was speedily put to death, and to John Rott and his descendants, in memory of the patriotic exploit, the citizens of Solothurn decreed the annual gift of a coat, in the city colors of red and white. On the Count of Kyburg, Solothurn took revenge by ravaging his estates; and during the lifetime of his successor the entire domain was divided between Solothurn and Bern.

This ruin of the ancient house of Kyburg aroused the animosity of other noble families against all who sought exemption from feudal bonds, and, confident of ability to crush both free cities and ambitious peasantry, the seignors multiplied their exactions until insurrections were the result. Then ecclesiastical and

## The Era of Sempach and Näfels

secular lords, assured of Austrian aid, joined to punish all who opposed their arbitrary sway, and in a short time war was again rampant over the land, massacres were perpetrated by the nobles, and castles destroyed by the people. Hostilities were brought to a crisis when, in resistance to new taxes imposed by Peter of Thorberg and the Count of Rothenburg, the castle of the one was razed to the ground and subjects of the other sought a defensive alliance with Luzern. The men of Luzern — in a chronic state of irritation since the Brandenburg Peace had compelled them to resume payment of revenues to Austria — attacked the custom-house at Rothenburg, and gave the privileges of burghership to the discontented people of the town of Sempach. Twenty threatening messages, received in succession by the confederates, failed to weaken their determination to assist the rebels, Bern alone standing aloof, on the ground that her truce with Austria had not expired.

Leopold III., of Austria, swearing vengeance upon all the confederates, united his forces with those of one hundred and sixty-seven seignors, and on the 9th of July, 1386, met the Swiss army near Sempach, in the canton of Luzern. The nobles, finding

*Battle of Sempach.*

their horses useless among the mountains, dismounted, cut the long peaks from their shoes that they might not become entangled in the high meadow grass, and closed in an apparently impenetrable phalanx, which bristled with pointed lances.

The fifteen hundred Swiss bore only boards for bucklers, and at the first charge many fell before the extended spears of the enemy. Undismayed, the peasants rushed forward a second time, but only to meet a similar repulse. The utter annihilation of the brave little band seemed inevitable, but suddenly the tide of battle turned, and winged Victory rested on the side of the patriots. The chronicled solution of this caprice of fortune was undisputed by early Swiss writers, though too romantic to be credited by modern historians. According to the ancient records, a knight of Unterwalden, named Arnold von Winkelried, heroically devoted his life to save his country, and at the third charge, extending his arms, with the words, "I will open a path to freedom; provide for my wife and children; honor my race!" he clasped as many as he could gather of the iron lances, and bore them to the earth. Over his prostrate body his comrades forced their way into the Austrian

## The Era of Sempach and Näfels 55

ranks, and, beneath Swiss maces, armored prince and knight fell to the ground, until six hundred of their number, with two thousand soldiers, had been slain by a band of fourteen hundred poorly-armed peasants. Thrice the Austrian banner sank, thrice was it raised again, until, Duke Leopold himself falling beside it, a disastrous flight ensued.

Thus, seventy-one years after Morgarten, the intrepid confederates again triumphed over Austria. Their leader, Gundoldingen, was slain in the battle, and their loss in numbers was great; but they were unsubdued. A truce for eighteen months was concluded with Austria, but so numerous were the acts of ill-faith committed on both sides during the period covered by the compact, that it be- *The "Bad* came notorious as the "Bad Peace." *Peace."* The spirit of animosity continued so intense, that in all Switzerland no man dared to display the peacock-feather (the symbol of the Austrian dukes); no peacock was permitted to live in the land; and it is recorded in Swiss annals that once a patriot shivered to fragments the drinking-glass he held, because through it, refracted sun-rays produced the variegated colors of the abhorred bird.

Believing that the power of Austria had been

broken at Sempach, Glarus, which since the treaty of 1352 had remained subservient to the Duke, now rose in rebellion; but in the closing months of the "Bad Peace," Austrian emissaries succeeded, through the treachery of citizens, in obtaining possession of the town of Wesen in the canton of Glarus, where they put to death the native garrison. Confederate assistance could not be expected while the mountain passes were blocked by snow, and the men of Glarus sought alone to redeem their city from the foe. The demands of the Austrians were peremptory. "You must obey Austria as serfs, have only such laws as your lord shall grant you, repudiate the bond with the confederate Swiss and serve against them, make compensation for the damage you have done, and expiate your misdeeds until you deserve the grace of the Duke." These terms Glarus refused to consider, and when all attempts at a compromise failed, the patriots, barely six hundred in number, stationed themselves at Näfels to encounter the Austrian army.

*Revolt of Glarus.*

*Battle of Näfels.*

Eleven simple stones, bearing only the date "1388," mark the spot where that handful of shepherds under Matthias Am Buel, landscaptain, kept in check the hosts of the enemy.

LAKE OF THUN.

## The Era of Sempach and Näfels 57

In the height of the struggle, shouts were heard upon the mountains, raised by thirty men of Schwyz hastening to assist their allies. The Austrians, ignorant of the number approaching, were startled and plunged into confusion. Their cavalry retreated, and their infantry fled in dismay, while the men of Glarus pursued, until twenty-five hundred of the enemy were slain, and many more drowned in the waters of the Linth.

This closed the list of battles against Austrian encroachments in the eight cantons,[1] Zug having been won by the men of Schwyz in 1364. The Duke, with both financial and military strength seriously impaired, willingly concluded a truce for seven years, which secured to the confederates all their acquisitions. Although private prerogatives of the house of Hapsburg as landed proprietors were guaranteed by Bern, Zurich, and Solothurn, with the acquiescence of the entire confederacy, the authority of Austria in all other respects was finally broken. The seven years' truce was in 1394 extended to twenty years. *Seven Years' Truce.*

Gradually the cities of the league multiplied their franchises, and purchased freedom from

---

[1] On the 5th of April, 1888, a monument was dedicated near Näfels to commemorate the victory.

the feudal jurisdiction of Austrian seignors. Luzern, Bern, and Zurich grew so prosperous that the privileges of their citizenship were sought by the neighboring nobility, who by this means acquired coveted prerogatives, one of which was the right to persecute the Jews.

Leopold IV. of Austria repeatedly attempted to sow dissensions among the confederates, but, Sempach Declaration or Frauenbrief. convinced of the importance of internal harmony, the cantons concluded, at Zurich, in 1393, a State compact, known as the Sempach Declaration. By special provisions therein recorded, federal sovereignty was strengthened, revengeful acts among members of the confederacy were prohibited, safety of intercourse and of commerce was insured, and unnecessary plunder of invaded territory was forbidden. Churches and convents were to be respected, but in time of war an enemy might be pursued even into churches. Women were never to be molested unless they took the offensive, hence this covenant was sometimes called the *Frauenbrief*, or "Woman's Charter."

The organization of the new state of Appenzell soon augmented the strength of the confederacy.

Appenzell.

A current tradition, of questionable historic

## The Era of Sempach and Näfels

accuracy, traces the settlement of Appenzell to a time when the devil, flying over the Sentis with a sackful of houses, tore a hole in the sack, and dropped the houses down in their present confusion; but a more credible reason for the habitation of the district is found in its proximity to the abbot's cell (*Abtzelle*), from which the name is derived.

On the extensive lands early granted to the Abbot of St. Gall, serfs of that ecclesiastic resided, who cultivated the ground and paid tithes of their harvests to the Abbot's bailiff. In this neighborhood freemen of the empire claimed the right to choose their own council, and were under the supervision of an imperial bailiff alone. By a gradual purchase of land the Abbots of St. Gall obtained from the Emperor jurisdiction over this adjacent territory, and then to the faithful abbey-people privileges were granted which raised them more nearly to the level of their neighbors.

In 1379, Kuno of Staufen became Abbot of St. Gall. He refused to confirm the franchises of the peasantry in either district, but increased their taxes, and enforced every claim of his early predecessors. When his bailiff caused a grave to be opened that he might obtain a coat, which had been the most valuable chattel of the dead tenant, the peasants rose in resistance to his tyranny, and attacked the Abbot's castle. Kuno obtained aid from six Swabian cities, reinstated his ejected officer, and refused heed to the request that his tenants might be permitted to nominate men from whom he should choose a bailiff. Then the Appenzellers sought a defensive alliance with the town of St. Gall, but, failing to secure this, asked aid of the confederates. Glarus and Unterwalden each sent two hundred men, and Schwyz promised support, though other members of the league stood aloof. When coercion was again attempted by the Abbot, his allies, to the number of five thousand, were totally overthrown in the defile of Speicher, **Battle on the Vögelinsegg.** by eighteen hundred shepherds of Appenzell, with their few allies from Schwyz and Glarus. This battle, on the hill Vögelinsegg, has been called "The Morgarten of Appenzell."

With success, the men of Appenzell gained courage, and the Abbot fled to implore aid of Austria. The Duke, Leopold IV., hesitated to render active assistance, but the influence of his nobility prevailed, and he made preparations for invading Appenzell with a formidable force. The peasants obtained an ally in Count

## The Era of Sempach and Näfels

Rudolf of Werdenberg, whose hereditary estates had been seized by Austria, and who, uniting his retainers with the troops of Appenzell, fought with them on foot, sharing their hardships, and inspiring them both by courage and counsel.

On a day in June, 1405, the Austrian army appeared, ascending the hill of Stoss, which leads to the heights of Appenzell. Made slippery by the abundant rain which was falling, the narrow pass proved a difficult path for mail-clad troops, into whose ranks bare-footed peasants hurled masses of heavy rock, increasing thus the confusion of their wavering advance. When the enemy had mounted the hill half-way, Count Rudolf gave the signal for assault, and a desperate conflict began. The rain had rendered the crossbows of the Austrians useless, but they fought valiantly, until put to rout by the sudden assault of a band of peasants who had been in ambuscade. The stories tell also of the sudden appearance of another army upon the heights above the pass, at sight of whom the enemy's courage failed, and they fled precipitately, unaware that the force whose advent discomfited them was composed of the women of Appenzell, clad in shepherds' frocks, who were advancing to share the fate appointed for their husbands and fathers.

*Battle of the Stoss.*

After this victory the Appenzellers destroyed more than sixty castles belonging to the Austrian nobility, and restored to the Count of Werdenberg his entire patrimony. Some victories over scattered forces from Appenzell were gained by troops attached to a band of Swabian nobles, and known as the League of St. George;[1] but the Duke of Austria had retreated to the Tyrol, and terms of peace were soon arranged which freed Appenzell from the jurisdiction of the Abbot of St. Gall. The district was then placed under the protection of the confederacy, although in the compact then framed Bern refused to co-operate, having already negotiated a private treaty for ten years with St. Gall.

*League of St. George.*

On the death of Leopold IV. of Austria (1411), Frederick of the Empty Pocket succeeded to the Hapsburg possessions. The strength of the confederacy was increasing; Bern had formed an alliance with Freyburg, and all the cantons were prompt, either secretly or openly, in proffering assistance to enemies of Austria. To prevent the total alienation of his dominions,

*Fifty Year Truce with Austria.*

---

[1] The Swabian League, or League of St. George, was derisively called the "Petticoat League," from the style of coat worn by members.

## The Era of Sempach and Näfels

Frederick concluded a peace for fifty years with the confederates, and by the terms of the treaty, Appenzell and Solothurn, as well as the cantons, were confirmed in their possession of all newly-acquired territory.

## CHAPTER VI

**THE COUNCIL OF CONSTANCE**

1414

LONG before the close of the middle ages, Europe was tossed in the tumult of religious controversy that culminated in the Reformation. Hallam characterizes the greater portion of the literature disseminated between the twelfth and sixteenth centuries, as "artillery levelled against the clergy," and the widespread luxury and immorality among the priestly class tended greatly to diminish the traditional reverence for its authority. The fourteenth century witnessed the so-called "Babylonish exile of the Papacy," at Avignon (1308–1378), and after the election of 1378, when Christendom beheld two rival pontiffs fulminating anathemas against each other, inquiry into the nature of the priestly office was instituted in a critical temper before unknown.

The council of Pisa sought, by the deposition of both Popes and the elevation of Martin V. to

## The Council of Constance

the ecclesiastical supremacy, to soothe the prevailing anarchy, but this proceeding served only to add fuel to the flames, and to sanction the pretensions of a third claimant for the papal chair.

For the consideration of these disputes and of kindred subjects, a General Council was summoned to convene at Constance. There gathered princes and nobles from all the kingdoms of Europe, with deputies from universities and representatives of monasteries. Their work was undertaken with zeal, the contending claimants for the papal chair were all deposed, and the Catholic world was once more united under a single head. This "most august ecclesiastical assemblage of the middle ages" also distinguished itself by breaking the spell that had formerly environed papal enactments, by the declaration that a council held authority in religious matters above the pontiff at Rome, — a tenet first propounded by Marsilius of Padua, in the foregoing century.

At this epoch, the doctrines of the English Wycliffe had become widely disseminated in Bohemia through the teachings of John Huss, "the John Baptist of the Reformation." Huss boldly proclaimed the necessity for holiness of life, and appealed from

*John Huss.*

the Pope to the Bible. By attacking the scandalous lives of the clergy, the reformer aroused a bitter personal animosity, whose first fruit was his excommunication. Driven by this sentence from his home in Prague, Huss was followed in his wanderings by many adherents, eager to receive his instructions, and when summoned to appear at the Council of Constance, his steps toward Switzerland were protected by an imperial safe-conduct.

Commanded by the Council to retract his heretical assertions, Huss steadily refused to comply, unless convinced of error through the Scriptures; and the Emperor Sigismund, noted as a sovereign "above the rules of grammar," was easily induced, despite his guarantee, to permit the imprisonment of the reformer. Every effort to force from Huss a recantation of his opinions proved ineffectual, and he steadfastly asserted his right to form private judgments, until led from the prison to the stake. On the forty-second anniversary of his birth, June 6, 1415, Huss was publicly burned to death, and his ashes thrown into the Rhine.[1]

[1] Huss used to say, in allusion to his own name, which in the Bohemian dialect signifies a goose, "The goose is a weak and tame creature, and cannot fly high, but stronger birds will follow it; falcons and eagles will soar aloft, breaking through all snares."

The following year the same sentence was executed upon Jerome of Prague, the learned and zealous associate of Huss.  *Jerome of Prague.*

Upon the death of King Wenceslaus of Bohemia, in 1419, the Emperor Sigismund laid claim to his dominions, but his succession was disputed by the Hussites, under their brave, though blind leader, John of Trocznow, surnamed "Ziska," whose skill in warfare baffled the efforts of Sigismund during fifteen years. The Hussites were divided into two sects, — the Calixtines or Utraquists, and the Saborites. The main point for which the Calixtines contended was the right of the laity to receive the cup in the communion, but they went beyond Huss in the claim that both elements were necessary in the administration of the sacrament. The Saborites, still more ultra than the Calixtines, sought an entire separation from the existing church. In 1433 an agreement was reached between the moderate party and the Council of Basle, *The Compactata.* and in a document known as the "Compactata," the Calixtines were granted many points for which they had long contended. Succeeding popes made efforts to annul the Compactata, but the Hussites strenuously insisted upon the prerogatives it sanctioned, until they finally attained a legal equality with the Catholics.

The summons to the three rival popes to appear before the Council of Constance was answered only by John XXII. Finding his position in the city an equivocal one, he fled thence to Schaffhausen, and sought refuge in the castle of the Duke of Austria, Frederick of the Empty Pocket. The protection afforded the deposed pontiff called forth against Frederick a bill of excommunication from the Council, which was followed by the ban of the empire, and a summons to all faithful imperial subjects to unite against Austria. The Swiss hesitated to obey; their treaty for fifty years having been recently concluded, Zurich, Zug, Luzern, and Glarus declared with the Waldstätten that the violation of this compact was impossible. But Bern, anxious to avail herself of the opportunity for acquisition of new territory, armed her troops, and when an imperial manifesto guaranteed to each canton permanent possession of whatever lands it might conquer from the enemy, she took the field without awaiting the concurrence of her allies. This aroused the jealousy of Zurich, who desired to share the prospective booty, and at length the entire confederacy, with the exception of Uri,

## The Council of Constance

followed the example of Bern. Aargau was quickly captured, the revolt of many vassals of Austria resulted in the loss of Thurgau, and misfortunes multiplied around Frederick until his resolution was broken, and, taking measures to prevent the escape of the Pope, he repaired to Constance, and tendered his submission to the Emperor. After months of humiliation the ban was removed, and the greater portion of the Duke's possessions were restored, though meanwhile his strong castle of Baden had been captured by the confederates and burned to the ground. This deed, committed just before the arrival of the imperial heralds with peace proclamations, excited the indignation of Sigismund, and he demanded that the Swiss should relinquish their conquests. They replied by quoting his previous decree with reference to the acquisition of territory, and Uri alone declined her share in the newly-won land, proposing that it should all be transferred to the Emperor in return for a guaranteed immunity from reprisals for violation of the truce with Austria. This proposition the other cantons refused to consider, but agreed to place their common acquisitions under the control of bailiffs who should be appointed by each canton in turn, and from whom, annu-

*War against Austria.*

ally-rendered accounts of their administration should be received by the confederacy. Thus **Free Bailiwicks.** were established common or so-called "free" bailiwicks, a travesty upon the word, as the districts possessed politically only such rights as were granted by the cantons.

These wars for the acquisition of territory, says the Swiss historian, Müller, "soiled the pure robe of the primitive confederacy." The century, which began with civil wars and foreign conquests ended in degrading mercenary service.

In the thirteenth century the opening of the St. Gothard pass had promoted friendly intercourse between the Waldstätten and their Italian neighbors, and a lively traffic in their respective articles of produce was long maintained.

In 1403 quarrels occurred among the merchants at the Valaisian fairs, and, in retaliation **Conflicts with Savoy.** for the seizure of their cattle, some men from Uri occupied the Duomo d'Ossola. The Duke of Milan had sold this valley to the Count of Savoy, and the latter's troops soon drove the Swiss peasants over the mountains; but the Savoyards had been guided to the valley by the Baron of Raron, a lord of Valais, who claimed citizenship with Bern,

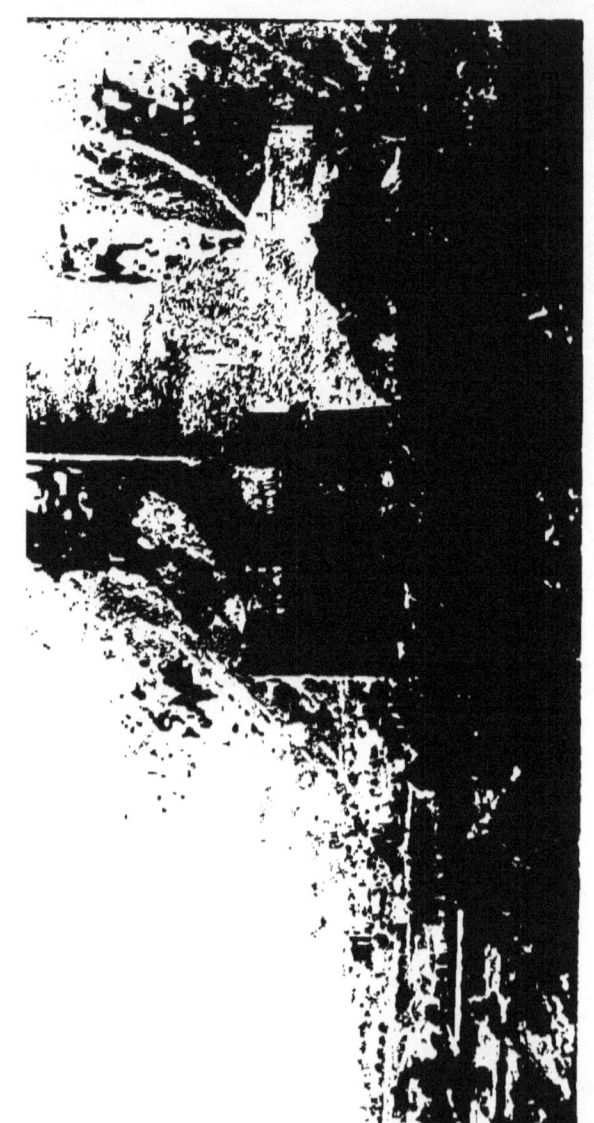

MARTIGNY: THE CASTLE.

## The Council of Constance

and complaints to that canton were accordingly entered by the aggrieved men of Uri and Unterwalden. Failing to receive satisfaction from this quarter, the Swiss then agreed to assist the oppressed vassals of the Baron of Raron in a revolt against their lord. For the purpose of exciting the peasantry and securing their co-operation, an ancient custom, called the "raising of La Mazze," was resorted to. At one end of a large club was carved a human face, which, to represent suffering, was surrounded with thorns; and this figure, named La Mazze, was exhibited on the highway. The crowds who gathered, questioned it unavailingly upon its grievance, until, designating the object of their antagonism, they inquired, "Art thou afraid of the Baron of Raron?" when the figure responded by an affirmative gesture. The man in attendance, who represented the master of "La Mazze," then harangued the assembled crowd, urging all who would fight for La Mazze to hold up their hands, and the mob, thus excited, was led through the country, pillaging the castles, and desolating the estates of the Baron.

Luzern joined Uri and Unterwalden, and supported Valais in these proceedings, but Bern opposed them, and suggested a settlement of differences by a Bernese diet. This method of pacification the Valaisians declined, and soon found themselves abandoned by Luzern, while Bern despatched against them an army of thirteen thousand men. At the village of Ulrichen six hundred resolute peasants, led by Thomas Riedie, almost exterminated the Bernese army, while (1419) near Münster another band inflicted upon their titled adversaries an equally overwhelming blow. The Baron of Raron was sent a fugitive into Savoy, but, through the mediation of Duke Amadeus VIII., a peace was concluded, which left the Swiss in possession of the Val d'Ossola and the Levantina.

<small>Battles of Ulrichen and Münster.</small>

But the Duke of Milan, jealous of these acquisitions, declared war against the confederates, and after a bloody conflict at Arbeddo, forced them to relinquish (1422) the new territory. A Schwyzer, named Peter Rysig, resolved to revenge this humiliation, and, having raised a force of six hundred men, crossed the mountains, and descended suddenly upon the inhabitants of the Val d'Ossola. The Milanese army, thirty thousand strong, marched to meet them; but when summoned to surrender, the valiant Rysig replied, "The Swiss are not conquered by

<small>Battle of Arbeddo.</small>

words!" and with heroic resolution encountered repeated assaults of the enemy. Stimulated by his enthusiastic bravery, twenty-two thousand confederates hurried to his aid; but the Duke of Milan won many through intrigue; and by the payment of thirty thousand florins and the grant of certain desirable commercial privileges, he ultimately secured possession of the Levantina.

. . . . . . .

Among the strangers gathered at Constance appeared a band of dark-complexioned, scantily-clad people, under a leader who called himself Duke Michael of Egypt. *Gypsies.* His followers, known as Zingari, or gypsies, pretended to be descendants of tribes of Lower Egypt, who had refused to receive Joseph and Mary. Having now become Christians, the band was on a seven-years' pilgrimage. It has been thought by philologists of a recent day that they were remnants of the race driven from India upon the overthrow of the dynasty of the Sultan of Ghaur.

## CHAPTER VII

### CIVIL WARS AND "THE EVERLASTING COMPACT"

#### 1436-1474.

SUBSEQUENT to the period of Frankish sovereignty, the peasants in the district of Rhetia
**Rhetia.** were governed by feudal lords, either secular or ecclesiastical, whose tyrannical rule caused frequent revolts. As early as 1396, defensive alliances against the despotism of their bishops were formed among subjects of the convents, who were known as "God's-House people"; and in 1424 the community of upper Rhetia, known as the "Gray League," from the color of the frocks worn by their deputies, secured from their seignors a guarantee of privileges. Upon the death of the Count of Toggenburg, a district extending from the Lake of Zurich to the Tyrol was claimed by various heirs, and to protect their hereditary rights the inhabitants united in a compact known as the "League of the Ten Jurisdictions." The localities occupied by the God's-

House league, the Gray league, and the league of the Ten Jurisdictions were then joined in a federal union, and by a modification of the designation bestowed upon the second league, gave the name of Grisons to the entire territory of Rhetia. *The Grisons.*

The Count of Toggenburg had been co-burgher with Zurich, and also with Schwyz; but after his death it was discovered that permanent jurisdiction over his vast estates had been left solely to Schwyz. Madame Elizabeth, the Count's widow, fearing a division of her property among various claimants, sought, by a liberal donation of lands, to gain the protection of Zurich. Hereupon Schwyz requested the heirs of the Count to forbid the alienation of any portion of the estates, and the two cities under their chief men, — Stüssi, burgomaster of Zurich, and Itel Reding, landammann of Schwyz, — were incited to acts of bitter antagonism. Each leader was ambitious to strengthen his own canton, at any expense. Schwyz sought the aid of Glarus, and, oblivious of more ancient bonds, stood ready for war; and Zurich, incited by jealousy and resentment, had already assumed arms, when the other confederates interfered. *Quarrel between Zurich and Schwyz.* A council was convened at Luzern, but adjourned after a session of four weeks, without having reconciled the antagonists. A second and a third assembly proved equally powerless, and Schwyz finally declared that she would accept no compromise. Then a general meeting was called at Bern, from whence messages were sent to the two wrathful cities, announcing the intention of the united confederacy to intervene should the terms proposed be rejected. Against such intervention Zurich protested, claiming the right of appeal to the empire; but in 1440 the troops of Uri and Unterwalden, in conjunction with those from Schwyz and Glarus, desolated her land with fire and sword, until, overpowered by the combination of hostile agencies, the city was forced to sign a disadvantageous peace. Stüssi then appealed to Austria for aid, and entered into an offensive and defensive league with the hereditary enemy of his land, offering to cede the city of Kyburg to Frederick V., who in 1440 had been elected Emperor of Germany. In the hats of the troops of Zurich, the red crosses worn by the Austrians supplanted the white confederate badges, and even the peacock's plume was occasionally displayed. Thus outraged by members of their own league, the other confederates

<small>Alliance between Austria and Zurich.</small>

hastened to join Schwyz in a declaration of war against Zurich and Austria; and in 1443 the army of Zurich was defeated at St. Jacob on the Sihl. In an attempt to rally his flying troops, the burgomaster, Stüssi, was struck down by the lance of a Schwyzer, when the furious soldiers, after tearing out his heart, madly rubbed their boots with portions of his flesh.

<small>Battle of St. Jacob on the Sihl.</small>

The confederates next besieged Baden and Rapperswyl; but failing to take the latter city, they agreed to a cessation of hostilities, and signed a treaty known as the "Rotten Peace," because so badly kept. Both parties then endeavored to acquire strength through outside alliances, and the Emperor asked aid of Burgundy and France. Philip the Good of Burgundy rejected every solicitation to open hostilities toward a people with whom his intercourse had long been both cordial and profitable; but France and Austria joined hands, and the Dauphin, "that troublesome heir to the throne," afterwards Louis XI., advanced upon Basle, with the rapacious mercenary troops known as Armagnacs.[1] A mere

<small>Invasion of Armagnacs.</small>

---

[1] So called from their leader, the Count of Armagnac, by whom they had been enlisted to serve in the war waged by Charles VII. of France against England.

handful of Swiss, numbering not more than two thousand, met his army near St. Jacob on the Birs, Aug. 26, 1444, and, with the cry "Our souls to God, our bodies to the Armagnacs," rushing dauntlessly into the fray, they fought with the heroic valor of their race until nearly all were slain. The remnant who escaped were disciplined with Spartan rigor, and proscribed throughout the land. But the victory was dearly bought by the French, and the victors dared not advance. "A more obstinate people cannot be found," wrote the Dauphin to Charles VII. A treaty[1] negotiated by Louis — the first ever concluded between the Swiss and the house of Valois — secured the confederacy against further molestation from France; but there were many fruitless attempts to effect a compromise in home interests before unity was restored. Stüssi and Itel Reding were both dead, the Emperor weary of the war, and through the arbitration of Louis, Elector-Palatine, and other princes, the foundation of a general peace was laid at Constance in 1450. The league of Zurich with Austria

*Battle of St. Jacob on the Birs.*

*Treaty with France.*

[1] In this treaty, negotiated between the French and the Swiss, at Ensisheim Oct. 28, 1444, the name "canton" first appears as a designation for individual states of the confederacy.

was pronounced contrary to the obligations of the confederacy, therefore null and void, and Toggenburg was left in the possession of a relative of the late Count, who subsequently sold it to the Abbot of St. Gall.

A ratification of the treaty consummated with France in 1444 not only riveted the friendly relations between that country and Switzerland, but induced Charles VII. to undertake the office of an arbitrator between Austria and the confederacy. <small>Truce with Austria.</small> Through his intervention, a truce between these habitual foes was arranged in 1459; but it was signed only to be broken, rearranged, and broken again.

Austrian knight-robbers plundered the baggage of merchants in Switzerland; the Swiss retaliated by laying waste the Austrian lands in Thurgau, Alsace, and the Schwarzwald, and besieging the town of Waldshut on the Rhine. A lengthy war seemed <small>Siege of Waldshut.</small> again imminent, until the influence of neighboring princes secured a peace in which Sigismund of Austria guaranteed to the Swiss all the territory they had conquered, and promised to ransom Waldshut by the payment of one hundred thousand florins. This sum he was unable to pay; the Emperor approved the contract, but contributed advice only, and the Duke made application for pecuniary aid to his ally, Louis XI., who, on the death of Charles VII., had succeeded to the throne of France.

Louis, with whom a chronic condition of bankruptcy was an inevitable result of his insatiable delight in intrigue, sug-gested Charles of Burgundy as the banker most opulent, and the ally most service-able. A double motive was always essential to this sovereign of France, of whom contemporaries said that "he slept with one eye closed during war, but kept both open in time of peace;" and Louis aimed at involving Charles in complications with the Swiss, hoping, by the promotion of strife between the confederacy and Burgundy, effectually to weaken an enemy whom he, both by deeply-laid schemes and through open hostilities, had striven in vain to humiliate.

*Intrigues.*

Charles of Burgundy, the "Napoleon of the middle ages," cherished secretly a project for the establishment of a new Burgundian kingdom, which should equal in extent the realm dismembered by Charlemagne. Realizing that these plans would be promoted by possession of the Rhineland, he readily agreed to advance the funds

*Austrian Lands mortgaged to Burgundy.*

BLUEBEARD'S CASTLE, NEAR INTERLAKEN.

solicited, together with an additional sum for the private use of the indigent Duke. At St. Omer, in May, 1469, the chief hereditary possessions of the Hapsburgs on both sides of the Rhine were mortgaged to Burgundy, "with full enjoyment of all rights of lordship and sovereignty," subject only to the pleasure of the Duke of Austria in redeeming them.

The debt to the Swiss was then discharged, and the Emperor disannulled the treaty of Waldshut. Charles intrusted the administration of his newly-acquired territory to Peter von Hagenbach, who had proved his devotion to the interests of Burgundy through years of service, but whose predilection for absolutism in the rule of the nobility rendered his conduct of affairs so tyrannical, that the borrowed appellation, "Scourge of God," distinguished him. Complaints of the severity of his government were sent to the Duke of Burgundy, but availed nothing, for, confident that his possession of the land would be permanent, Charles had resolved to subject it to a rule more arbitrary than that of the Hapsburgs. When his designs became evident to the free cities of Alsace, they determined to unite in a defiance of the authority thus gravely menacing their freedom; and, as

*Hagenbach.*

the readiest means of effecting their purpose, they agreed to furnish Sigismund with the means of redeeming his property.

But the designs of the Duke of Austria, in entering upon the contract with Burgundy, had reached beyond the circle of protection afforded by the alliance. Sigismund discerned in his valorous ally, not a mediator between Austria and the Swiss, but a subjugator of those hereditary antagonists of his house. By the terms of the league of St. Omer, the Swiss were warned against molesting the Austrians, who were thenceforth under Burgundian protection, although, unless hostilities were provoked by overt or secret acts toward his ally, the relations between Charles and the confederacy were to continue on the same amicable footing as formerly. When, therefore, Sigismund demanded that "a great and good army" should be despatched against the Swiss, the Duke replied that any act of aggression on his part would be wholly inconsistent with the relations existing between Burgundy and the confederacy, and only in case of provocation from the latter would a hostile attitude toward them be justifiable.

Failing in every effort to achieve his purpose through his alliance with Burgundy, Sigismund then secretly projected another intrigue, and again sent emissaries to the Court of France. At the time of the first Austrian embassy, the Swiss, fearing some arrangement inimical to their interests, had also despatched ambassadors, to mediate, if necessary, in their favor. These men, the Diesbachs, prominent citizens of Bern, had ingratiated themselves with the French king, and Louis, who never permitted an opportunity for the exercise of craft to escape him, beguiled them into acting as his instruments upon their return home. When the second proposition from Sigismund was received, it was combined in the mind of Louis with the design of inveigling the Swiss into his alliance, and presenting them as a strong bulwark of defence against Burgundy. Sigismund's offensive designs toward the Swiss were subordinated to these projects, and the French king, through the influence he was secretly, and by bribery, able to exert at Bern, consummated his scheme of uniting Austria, France, and the confederacy in an alliance antagonistic to Burgundy. The union promised nothing to the Swiss, and the consent of a majority of the cantons was at first withheld; but French gold at length pre-

*[margin: The Diesbachs.]*

*[margin: League between France, Austria, and the Swiss.]*

vailed to influence all save Unterwalden; and one hundred and fifty-nine years after Morgarten, eighty-eight years after Sempach, an "eternal covenant" was signed at Feldkirch, between Austria and the confederacy, under the guarantee of France. In this compact, Sigismund renounced all claim in Switzerland to former Austrian prerogatives, and exchanged with the cantons pledges of friendship and support. He covenanted to redeem the mortgaged lands with gold furnished by Alsace, and a general defiance to Burgundy was declared.

# CHAPTER VIII

## WAR WITH BURGUNDY

### 1474-1475

CHARLES THE BOLD had long been suspicious of clandestine dealings on the part of Sigismund, but the envoys from Austria indignantly repudiated every implication of treachery, and denied the intimation that their sovereign's intercourse with the French might be inimical to the interests of Burgundy. The fidelity of the Swiss was presumably secured, for the Duke's officers in Alsace had received strict commands to preserve inviolate every prerogative claimed by the confederacy.

When, therefore, the Alsatian towns advanced the sum for payment of the mortgage, spurred to action by a report that at Trèves the Duke had been crowned King of Burgundy, Charles refused to receive the proffered gold, or to relinquish possession of the territory. In a revolt at Breisach, Hagenbach was seized and carried before a tribunal which included some

Swiss officials. Accused of many private misdemeanors, as well as of violating the franchises of the people under his government, he was cruelly tortured, condemned, and publicly beheaded (1474). Charles, although enraged, postponed his retaliation while occupied with affairs incident to the extension of his dominions on the Rhine.

*Death of Hagenbach.*

Louis, in the meantime, had won over the Emperor Frederick V., who, as soon as affairs between Austria and Burgundy had reached an open rupture, summoned the confederates to take part in the approaching conflict. At Bern, where executive authority for the confederacy had been vested, a message to the Duke of Burgundy was prepared, and inserted, after the usual custom, in a split in the herald's staff. It announced that, in obedience to the command of the Emperor, and on account of the invasion of Sigismund's territory, whose adherents they declared themselves, the Swiss were thenceforth enemies to their quondam ally, and in substantiation of this announcement they were ready to execute hostile purposes against him "by slaying, by burning, by plundering, in the day or in the night."

*Message to Burgundy.*

Thus far, the King of France had executed with perfect success the scheme he had so carefully concocted. He had succeeded in providing himself with valiant, skilful, and reliable troops, secretly under his control, through their greed of gold, while ostensibly they were marshalled against the foe of the empire, in obedience to their duty as imperial subjects.

Before the letter to Charles had reached its destination, troops from Bern, with a small force from Freyburg and Solothurn, had set forth upon an expedition into the enemy's territory. With five hundred Austrian cavalry the army numbered about eight thousand men, all of whom adopted as their badge the white cross of the Swiss confederacy. The fort- <small>Attack upon Héricourt.</small> ress of Héricourt, in Franche-Comté, was besieged, and a Burgundian force, under Henri de Neuchâtel, governor of the district, advanced to its relief. The savage assault of the Swiss scattered this army in immediate flight, and secured the capitulation of the fortress. Louis of France was profuse in the expression of pleasure and commendation, but the more tangible aid of French troops was still delayed, and when the money promised for the payment of the Swiss soldiers failed to be delivered, Bern became uneasy, and, with five other cantons, expressed openly her suspicions of the good faith of the French ally. Complications increased when Yolande, Queen-Regent of Savoy, who had been in alliance with both Burgundy and the confederacy, allowed the passage through her territory of Lombard troops on their way to join the army of Charles the Bold. The demand sent forth from Bern, that Savoy should dissolve her treaty with the Duke, on the ground of his antagonism both to the empire and to France — to whose king Yolande was sister — was met by many remonstrances from the ingenious queen, whose agents, profiting by the divided opinions in the cantons, concerning the treaty with France, endeavored to stir up strife in the confederacy. Yolande courted, and obtained for herself and for Charles, the alliance of Galeas Sforza, Duke of Milan; but this support failed to prove the safeguard for Savoy that the Queen had anticipated. The demand that she should renounce the alliance with Burgundy and unite her strength with that of the confederacy was repeated, and upon the receipt of her absolute refusal a severe punishment was threatened, and subsequently executed.

In the conduct of these affairs, Bern, influenced by a private retainer from Louis, had frequently acted upon her own responsibility,

## War with Burgundy

without waiting for the sanction of the other cantons. As hired troops in the service of the King of France, the confederates considered themselves summoned to the battlefield at his command, and with sublime confidence in the assertion, "A handful of Swiss is a match for an army," they feared no foreign foe. But they regarded their compact as one for mercenary service, without responsibility, and they were unaffected by incidental circumstances of the war, that might be of supreme importance either to Austria or the empire. Sigismund's call for troops to protect Alsace was disregarded; but when the safety was threatened of a small force from Bern and Solothurn, which, on a predatory excursion, had entered Burgundian territory, the alarum from Bern summoned from Luzern, Schwyz, and other cantons, swift aid to meet the emergency. This danger past, the Diet refused to continue their provision for reinforcing the army; but Diesbach, who held command of troops already in the field, projected a private expedition into the Jura, with the aim of possessing himself of territory long coveted by Bern. At Orbe, a castle — belonging to the house of Chalons, which paid allegiance to Burgundy — was attacked and taken, although the garrison resisted until every man had been slain. The surrender of the town speedily followed, and the terrified inhabitants of neighboring districts offered slight opposition to the capture of places of inferior strength. The army then marched homeward, greeted everywhere along their route with hospitable entertainment from the trembling populace, who sought thus to propitiate those whom they had formerly regarded as allies and protectors.

Meanwhile Louis XI. had found it politic to send troops of his own into the field, but he continued to entreat the Swiss auxiliaries, whom he characterized as "the bravest of Christians," to hasten to his assistance. A call for troops came from Sigismund also, who complained that he had been unable to obtain from the Swiss that aid in the prosecution of the war against Burgundy which the terms of their treaty had authorized him to anticipate. In the Diet summoned at Luzern, to deliberate upon the response to this imperial demand, the majority of cantons voted against compliance with its terms, and reiterated their assertion that the compact bound them only to the duties specified in their treaty with France.

While the discussion upon this matter was pending, Alsace was threatened by a Burgundian

THE JUNGFRAU.

army, and the inhabitants, in desperation, sent envoys to the Swiss, offering, with their "eternal gratitude," what proved more influential with those mercenary neighbors, — a large recompense in money for troops whose very name had become potent to terrify the enemy. Bern promised aid, and a force under command of Diesbach was soon on its way to the imperilled district. This expedition proved the final one in which the veteran statesman engaged, for, while weakened from an accidental wound, he was attacked by cholera, and died after a short illness. *Death of Diesbach.* A tablet above his tomb, in the church of St. Vincent, at Bern, records that he was the author of the French alliance and of the pension system. Soon after his death a pestilence ended the campaign, in which the Swiss had been mainly victorious.

During this period, Yolande of Savoy, unaided by her ally, the Duke of Milan, had anticipated the execution of the vengeance threatened by Bern. Under the pretext of military necessity, Bernese troops seized places in the Valais, and looked with covetous eyes upon adjacent territory. A missive addressed to the other confederates asserted that the treacherous conduct of the Count of Romont, who had plotted to expel the Swiss from the Valais, was sufficient reason for despatching another army into Savoy; but before notice of the project could be received by their allies, the Bernese troops set forth upon the expedition. Contriving to arrive at Morat under cover of darkness, they demanded the immediate submission of the garrison; a majority in the town, paralyzed by terror of the Swiss arms, voted to yield, and with daylight the exultant band marched toward Estavayer. The commandant at that place, a knight descended from the founders of the town, threatened death to any one suggesting surrender; but while an assault upon the walls was in progress, a hanging rope above the margin of the lake furnished means whereby a Swiss soldier gained the ramparts of the town, and, swiftly followed by comrades, diverted the attention of the gateway defenders, until an entrance there had been forced. A massacre and plunder ensued, disgraceful to the annals of Switzerland, and many misfortunes that subsequently befell Bern were regarded as retributive justice for "the bad day of Estavayer."

*Expedition into Savoy.*

*"The Bad Day of Estavayer."*

Insubordination among the troops was a natural result of the licence permitted on this occasion, and the commanders found themselves continually importuned for redress by those whose possessions had been despoiled, or whose rights had been invaded by the soldiery. But onward swept the destroying bands, Terror flying before them. Yverdon, Orbe, Les Clées, were occupied after short sieges; and, reinforced by troops from other cantons, gathered at the summons of the diet, the army approached Geneva.

Toward this city Bern had cherished a special grudge, since her envoy, Diesbach, had there suffered insult on his return from Paris. The origin of the trouble might be traced to the restrictions placed by Louis XI. upon the right of transit through France to Geneva, when fairs in that city had attracted French merchants. In consequence of those restrictions the trade of Geneva had been diverted to Lyons, whereupon Savoy had prohibited passage through her territory, making exception only in favor of the Swiss. Geneva requested the intervention of Bern on her behalf, and the failure of a satisfactory adjustment of affairs was ascribed to Diesbach, then ambassador to France, who was believed to have been bribed to act in the interest of Louis. Consequently his arrival in Geneva was the signal for an affront, for which Bern had demanded large indemnity.

*Geneva threatened.*

The army marched along the shore of the lake, took quiet possession of Morges, and advanced toward Geneva. That city, destitute of fortifications and abounding in wealth, was in abject terror at the approach of the foe. Deputies sent to propitiate the invaders offered hostages for the payment of twenty-six thousand crowns, and the Swiss, like Alaric the Goth, withdrew their rapacious bands, whose detailed deeds in this campaign might rank with those of the savage hordes that threatened ancient Rome.

Lausanne was menaced, but secured herself against attack by the payment of a heavy ransom, and abasement from a condition of almost entire freedom under Savoy to one of vassalage to the Swiss. The army then turned homeward, having in three weeks secured dominion over all of Savoy north of the Alps. Conjointly with Freyburg, which in the greater portion of the campaign had acted in conjunction with Bern, the Swiss then established garrisons throughout the district, and Rudolf von Erlach, the younger, was established at Lausanne, to act, in co-operation with the deputy from Freyburg, as vice-regent of the conquered territory.

# CHAPTER IX

### GRANDSON, MORAT, AND NANCY

#### 1475-1477

DURING months of military activity on the part of the Swiss, no communication had been received from the French king, and when the half-yearly pensions failed to appear, Bern realized that her influence would not long be effective in maintaining a war so unpopular with the majority of cantons. Through the diplomacy of Rudolf of Hochberg, Margrave of Neuchâtel, whose estates lay open to incursions from both combatants, a truce between the Burgundians and Swiss was projected; but the negotiations were checked by a demand from Charles that full restitution should be allowed for injuries inflicted either upon himself or his allies.

An increasing dissatisfaction with the conduct of affairs became manifest in the diet, and from Bern and Luzern letters were sent to the Swiss ambassador at Paris, Jost von Silenen, reminding him of the omission of the payment promised by France, and urging the exertion of every influence to effect a prompt fulfilment of the contract between the King and the confederates. The reply of the ambassador brought assurances of Louis's good faith, and emphatic reassertions of his resolution to adhere to his covenant with the Swiss and to maintain his antagonism to Burgundy "at the risk of life and of power."

But before anything beyond promises of aid had been received, the Swiss garrison at Yverdon was summoned to defence against an attack from the Burgundians; and although, aided by other confederates, they forced the enemy to retire, the attitude of neighboring places during that crisis revealed the disposition of the entire region to rise in revolt. As the French money was reported to be coming that way, a necessity for more securely fortifying the newly-acquired territory became evident.

Charles, aware that the war was unpopular with the majority of cantons, believed that weakness and disunion would attend any efforts to prolong hostilities, could he once succeed in humiliating the military pride of the Swiss nation. Realizing the importance of impressing the enemy, at the first encounter, with the strength and valor of the Burgundian army, his arrangements were completed with deliberation, while the confederates, ignorant of his designs, vacillated in purpose, and marched from point to point in anticipation of attack. Too late to fortify their possessions along his route, they realized that Bern was the enemy's objective point; Lausanne and other towns were swiftly secured by the invading army, and in a few days the entire territory recently taken from Savoy was lost to the confederacy.

The deliberations of the diet assembled at Bern were interrupted by tidings of these calamities. Orders for troops, delayed on account of the lack of unanimity among the cantons, were now hastily issued, and Bern announced her intention of taking the field at once, in conjunction with Freyburg and Solothurn. Messengers were despatched to the other cantons, to conjure them, with a torrent of entreaties, to hasten, "without delay, with all their power, and without any stop," and promising, for immediate aid, "recompense in all future time, without sparing life or prosperity."

At first, even these urgent calls met slight response from the allies, who reflected that the parsimony of Bern had led them into a war against which the greater number of cantons had protested, and, although troops were ordered to assemble, it remained with the council at Luzern to decide upon the number to be sent into the field. But soon the progress of events left no room for doubt of the real extremity to which Bern was reduced, and then the action of the confederates was prompt and decided.

The Duke of Burgundy had advanced to Grandson. That town had been strengthened by the garrison from Yverdon, who, barely in time to escape the rapidly-approaching foe, received commands to evacuate their first position. But, even with this addition, the force at Grandson was insufficient for defence; the town was quickly taken, and its defenders chased into the castle, where they were besieged by the Burgundian army.

*Siege of Grandson.*

The council at Bern remained in session day and night. Messages were sent to Louis XI., expressing continued confidence in his promises, but urging the great and immediate need of active aid from France. Requests for help were also sent to Austria, but failed to elicit even a sympathetic response from Sigismund. The Emperor Frederick, always famous for his readiness to leave his allies in the lurch, had deserted the confederates openly, and without a pretence of excuse. He had concluded a treaty with Charles, in which no reference was made, either to France, Austria, the towns of Alsace, or the Swiss confederacy. This treaty, "remarkable for its omissions," had been ratified by a promise of the hand of Mary of Burgundy, the only child of the Duke, for Maximilian of Austria, the Emperor's son.

The little force at Grandson maintained a brave defence in the face of many disasters, until they became convinced that there was no hope of succor from the confederates. *Surrender of Grandson.* Then an unconditional surrender was forced from them, and, four hundred strong, they were doomed to expiate the massacres of Estavayer and Orbe. Sentence of death was executed upon all; many were hung upon the trees around Grandson, others drowned in the waters of the lake. Too late, their brother-confederates advanced to the rescue, —an army of nineteen hundred men, including troops from Freyburg and from Solothurn. Their route to Grandson lay past the castle of Vauxmarcus, owned by a vassal of the Count of Neuchâtel. At the summons of the Duke of Burgundy it had yielded to him, and a body of his archers now formed the garrison. Near at hand, the main army of Burgundians were strongly intrenched, and might have awaited in security the attack of the Swiss. But, believing that it was the aim of the confederates to dispute his passage to Neuchâtel, Charles made an effort to secure the mountain-pass over which the route lay. Some detachments from Bern, eager for conflict, hastened forward to occupy a position of advantage at the side of the pass, and the Burgundians vainly endeavored to dislodge them. Charles then resorted to artifice; and, to lure the enemy into a position where the superior numbers of his own troops might prove more effective, he drew off the latter in a pretended retreat. The over-confident Swiss fell readily into the snare, and soon found themselves surrounded by the enemy. The conflict then waxed desperate; but at a critical moment loud blasts from the mountain-side startled the combatants and reanimated the confederates, who recognized the familiar tones of the horns of Uri and Unterwalden. The Burgundians, panic-stricken, mistook a sudden motion of their cavalry for the signal to retreat, and, raising the cry, "Sauve qui peut!" they fled precipitately, while Charles made vain attempts to rally them. Ere long the field was deserted by Burgundian troops, and, almost by force, attendants urged the Duke away.

*Battle of Grandson.*

His camp — a luxurious city — greeted the astonished gaze of the victors. The old chronicler, Philippe de Commines, has described in glowing terms the treasures there exhibited. With the intention of holding court the next season in Savoy, the Duke had brought with him the crown regalia, and ceremonial appurtenances of his court. The sword of state, incrusted with precious gems, immense diamonds, treasure manuscripts, beautiful tapestries, and robes of costliest fabric, were articles of booty, with six hundred standards, ten thousand pack horses, and arms in corresponding quantity. Gold is reported to have been divided by the hatful; but some authorities maintain that any private appropriation of the plunder was forbidden, under the severest penalty, and that only after several years had elapsed, and a full inventory of the captured wealth had been completed, was division and distribution made.

One of the diamonds, after passing through many hands, was finally purchased for the papal crown, another rested in the treasury of Vienna, while a third was returned to India, whence it had come.

After the victory of Grandson, Vaud, which on the approach of Charles had been overrun by Savoy, was reoccupied by the Swiss, and French-speaking districts came thus for the first time into permanent contact with the confederacy.

The influence of France procured the subsequent restoration of a large portion of the territory, when the Duke of Savoy renounced authority previously exercised over Freyburg.

Far from believing his fortune ruined by the defeat of his troops, Charles immediately began preparations for another struggle, issued commands for the return of all fugitives, levied throughout his dominions the tax of every sixth penny, and compelled the enlistment of every sixth man. Recruits were also raised in Italy, where arms and equipments were purchased. The neighborhood of Lausanne was selected as the locality most advantageous for a camp, and was promptly occupied by a force of twenty thousand men, who were placed under rigid discipline. Charles declared his determination to recover his reputation or die in battle, and from this purpose of seeking another encounter with the Swiss, neither counsel nor warning could dissuade him.

By this time doubts were freely expressed concerning the fidelity of the ally who so often and so vehemently had declared his resolution "to live and die with his most loved, most cherished friends, the Swiss." Again the confederates despatched urgent messengers to France. Louis renewed his protestations of devotion and his promises of aid, which had been delayed, he declared, only by complications in which he had hitherto been involved at home. By repeated promises, flattery, and bribes, the council at Bern was persuaded again to exert an influence in the confederacy on behalf of France, although the passing months failed to bring any tangible evidence of good faith from their perfidious ally. Ere long, with an army vastly superior in numbers to the one encountered at Grandson, the Burgundians threatened Bern. Between Lausanne and Bern lay Morat, a town acquired during the war, and, consequently, regarded with a degree of indifference by a large proportion of confederates. By Bern, however, it was looked upon as "a bulwark of the territory," and its defence was resolved upon. Adrian von Bubenberg, an honest and able patriot, was selected to command the place. He accepted the responsibility upon condition of being endowed with authority to enforce unlimited obedience to his orders, and then exacted an oath from the garrison that surrender should never be suggested. Every preparation to defend the town was completed under Bubenberg's direction, and fre-

*Morat.*

quent letters to the council of Bern kept that body informed of the condition of Morat, while the confederates were urged to defer sending reinforcements, until an army should be gathered of sufficient strength to prevent the possibility of disaster.

Bubenberg soon found that the siege was likely to be protracted. The army of Burgundy, augmented, according to the most reliable authorities, to forty thousand men, arrived before Morat on the 9th of June, Charles anticipating a speedy reduction of the town and a swift advance upon Bern. That the vigilance of his garrison might never be relaxed, Bubenberg ordered the gates of the city to be left open, and frequent sallies against the enemy were executed without serious damage to either side. The cannon of Burgundy proved more effective for injury, and several breaches in the city walls induced Bubenberg to despatch a messenger to hasten the confederate aid. These heralds found no lack of sympathy among the allies; whatever jealousies had existed were forgotten, and even Unterwalden, the last canton to yield consent to the war, now rang her alarm bells and lighted signal fires.

*Siege of Morat.*

When the relieving army reached Bern, the

entire city was illuminated, and before every house upon their route stood refreshment tables. Little time could be allowed the weary troops to recover from the exhaustion of their march, for messages telling of immediate peril at Morat had been received, and crowds of weeping women urged forward the rescuing bands. The advice of Ulric Kätzy, landammann of Schwyz, was accepted, and, avoiding the direct route by which the enemy might anticipate their approach, the army crossed the hills to meet the main body of Burgundians.

René of Lorraine had joined the Swiss, and the army, augmented by his troops, marched forward, nearly forty thousand strong. Scouts had given the Duke of Burgundy early information of their approach, and for hours his army had been posted in battle array, anticipating attack. But as the day wore on, and the reconnoitring band sent forward by the Swiss had retired out of sight, Charles apprehended no immediate attack, and permitted his weary troops to lay aside their arms.

The confederates had halted in the woods while prayers were recited by a soldier in each band. During many hours rain had been falling heavily, but as the men rose from their knees the sun burst through the clouds, and

John of Halwyl, waving his sword above his head, shouted, "See! God will shine upon our victory!" Under the inspiring influence of these words, the troops rushed forward, startling the enemy from their relaxation. Charles had no time for arranging his troops in the order in which they had been trained to fight. With the battle-cry, "Grandson!" the Swiss resisted every charge of the Burgundians, hurling back one division after another upon those forming in the rear. The garrison of Morat made a sally at the same time, and, in the words of a Swiss chronicler, "the smiting and fighting spread from the lake to the heights."

*Battle of Morat.*

Fifteen thousand of the Duke's army lay dead upon the field, and still he fought bravely with a free company of English. At length, every manœuvre having failed, he gave orders to fall back to a more favorable position. But, to the demoralized army, this command was equivalent to a signal for retreat, and over every hillside, in wild confusion, fled the dismayed soldiers, pursued by the triumphant Swiss, until the land ran red with blood, and the lake had engulfed hundreds. It was impossible justly to estimate the Burgundian loss, but it has been computed at twenty-two thousand.

Heralds of victory hastened to circulate among the confederates the glorious tidings, and a joyous chiming of bells closed that memorable day among the Alps.[1]

Charles the Bold had been borne from the battlefield in the press of his flying troops. He arrived, toward morning, at Morges, on Lake Geneva, where he was met by Yolande of Savoy, to whom he declared his still inflexible purpose of continuing the contest. The estates of the "Two Burgundies," convened at Salines in an eloquent address from their prince, were exhorted to provide for the safety of their homes, and promised to supply whatever resources were necessary.

The victorious and exultant confederates, raised to the summit of military renown, were recipients from every side of congratulations and offers of alliance.

---

[1] Nine years later, Freyburg and Bern combined to raise a building over the spot where the remains of those who fell in the battle of Morat had been deposited. This was several times rebuilt during succeeding centuries, but in 1778 the latest edifice was destroyed by the Burgundian division of the French army, and, the earth having been washed away by rain, bleached remains were exposed to view. Byron visited the place in 1816 and mentions the few bones remaining from which he ventured to bring away "as much as may have made a quarter of a hero." Since the poet's visit, the remaining fragments have been buried under an obelisk of marble.

At a diet held at Freyburg, an embassy of congratulation from France was received. After having eloquently expatiated upon the satisfaction of their monarch in the recent victory at Morat, the envoys reiterated the desire of the King that the war be continued until the enemy's strength should be annihilated, and protested that it was the purpose of France to unite with the Swiss for this end. The confederates expressed their gratification in learning that Louis was at length willing to enter upon the war, but, before further action on their part, they desired to call the attention of the King to the pension of eighty thousand francs which had been forfeited by France through her failure to come to the aid of her allies in the recent campaign.

It was proposed that an embassy should be sent to confer with the King of France upon this matter, and the heroes of Grandson and Morat were delegated for the mission: Waldmann from Zurich, Kätzy and Reding from Schwyz, Herterstein and Hassfurter from Luzern, Halwyl and Bubenberg from Bern, Diesbach and Albert von Silenen as representatives of the other cantons. At Paris they were received with every honor, and, during their stay, which lasted

*Embassy to France.*

many weeks, a continual round of festivities entertained them. Louis was profuse in his expression of grateful sentiments toward the Swiss, and knew where to emphasize his words by private gifts; but when the settlement of his indebtedness to the confederacy was discussed there appeared serious discrepancies in the estimates made by the two nations. A compromise was, however, arranged, Louis having reason still to consider liberality toward his allies the most politic course, and the conferences were closed with repeated assurances from the confederates of their faithful adherence to France.

At the last Swiss diet, René of Lorraine had been accorded a position of honor, and his petition for help in releasing his duchy from the grasp of Burgundy had obtained a hearing, although no positive assurances of aid had been given. Nancy, the capital of Lorraine, had passed from the possession of René into that of Burgundy, and from Burgundy back to Lorraine, as fortune had favored, or deserted its King, during the recent months. The Swiss fearing that René, if abandoned, might now be forced into an alliance with Burgundy, detrimental to their interests, agreed to furnish him a force of eight thousand men,

*René of Lorraine.*

stipulating for a portion of the promised wages in advance, and reliable pledges for the remainder. Thus were the first avowedly mercenary troops furnished by the Confederacy, the French pension being regarded as only the seal of a friendly alliance between the countries. The disorderly and riotous conduct of the Swiss bands gave René good reason to regret his bargain, and only through a free disbursement of gold was control over them secured. With these troops he advanced to the relief of Nancy, besieged a second time by the Burgundians. Having received messages of encouragement from their King, the garrison obstinately refused to surrender, although reduced to the extremities of famine. The Duke of Burgundy, having seen the prize almost within his grasp, would not withdraw at the approach of the Swiss, and the troops who could boast of Grandson and Morat, pressing eagerly forward, with triumphal blasts from their horns, charged upon the foe. At that moment the Italian Campobasso, with the troops under his command in the Burgundian army, treacherously deserted to René. The Duke, seeing disaster and defeat for the third time inevitable, chose death rather than dis-

*marginalia: 1476. Battle of Nancy.*

grace. Plunging into the midst of the surging bands, giving no quarter, seeking none, he charged wildly forward. The battle raged furiously, and ere it was ended Charles the Bold, the Rash, the Warlike, the Terrible, had fallen! his body pierced by many wounds, but the death-blow given by the halberd of a Swiss soldier.[1]

[1] An ancient chronicle records, —
"Bei Grandson das Gut,
Bei Minten (Morat) den Mut,
Bei Nancy das Blut."

# CHAPTER X

### LEAGUE OF THIRTEEN DISTRICTS

#### 1478-1499

IN the exhilaration of their triumph over Burgundy, no foe seemed formidable to the Swiss soldiers, and a desire to exhibit their military prowess often led to the provocation of hostilities with neighboring powers. An instance of this was exhibited in 1478, when, in retaliation for the act of some Milanese who had cut timber without permission, in a forest belonging to Uri, the young men of that canton plundered several Italian villages. Despite remonstrances from members of the league, the government of Uri then declared war. Immediately the Duke of Milan sent an army into the field, and the confederates, unwilling to desert one of their number, were compelled to send troops to the Ticino.

*Incursions into Italian Territory.*

It was midwinter, and the advance-guard of Swiss — in number about six hundred — flooded the meadows in front of their encampment, at the village of Giornico, and over the quickly-frozen water advanced on skates to meet the enemy. With uncertain steps the Milanese moved forward, but their swaying ranks of fifteen thousand men, unable to obtain secure footing in any spot, were quickly overcome, and their blood dyed red the snow, as they sought escape from the swiftly-gliding Swiss. The "glorious day of Giornico" (Dec. 28, 1478) secured for the confederates a large indemnity from Milan, and the possession of the Levantina, and the Brugiasco, upon condition of the annual gift of a wax-candle to the Duomo of Milan.  *Battle of Giornico.*

Other results of the Burgundian wars, and of the sudden and unequal distribution of wealth that followed, were widely demoralizing. A love of an exciting and lawless life had been engendered, and soldiers, statesmen, and prelates began to frequent the springs of Baden, where music and games beguiled the hours, but where the Spartan traits of the early confederates were forgotten.

Around the Swiss league gathered a class of allies known as *zugewandte Orte*, or associate districts. They were connected with the cantons by a subordinate alliance, and were under obligations to  *"Associate Districts."*

obey the Swiss diet in matters relating to war, or to foreign treaties, while remaining independent in minor affairs. In the fifteenth century, the confederates were thus in alliance with thirteen towns or districts, among which St. Gall, Mülhausen, Schaffhausen, and Appenzell were prominent.

As opportunity for individual cantonal aggrandizement occurred, jealousies and distrust were fostered. Allies were aided only when the service seemed reciprocally profitable, and internal dissensions began to eradicate the feeling of mutual dependence that had been the glory and strength of the young confederacy.

Between the city cantons, Bern, Zurich, and Luzern, and the country cantons, which included **Jealousies.** Schwyz, Glarus, Uri, Unterwalden, and Zug, the spirit of jealousy was prominently active, and in 1481, when Bern proposed the admission of Freyburg and Solothurn into the confederacy, antagonism was openly manifested. At a Diet held at Stanz, **Diet of Stanz.** the opposition to the proposition offered by Schwyz, Uri, and Unterwalden was so strenuous that even a dissolution of the confederacy seemed imminent, and the delegates from the cities seeking admission withdrew their applications. Suddenly, in the midst of the angry assembly, appeared a tall and slender figure, venerable, but still vigorous. All rose to their feet and received, reverently, the unexpected guest, Nicholas-of-the-Flue, the hermit of Oberwalden. A belief in the wonderful sanctity of his life was universal, and his words came with almost sacred authority as he urged the confederates to acts of peace and concord. "You have become strong," he said, "through union; will you now separate for the sake of wretched booty? Cantons, remember how Freyburg and Solothurn have fought by your side; and freely receive them into your *Bund*. Beware of internal discord! Far be it from any to take gold as the price of the fatherland!"

An hour later all was harmony. Freyburg and Solothurn were received, and a covenant was accepted, in which the constitution of the Swiss confederation was first definitely settled by the associated members. The covenant of 1291, the *Pfaffenbrief* of 1370, and the Edict of Sempach (1393) were all ratified, and amendments suggested by Nicholas-of-the-Flue were incorporated with these earlier ordinances. Interference by any canton with the internal affairs of another was strictly forbidden, but should insurrections occur, the

<small>Covenant of Stanz.</small>

allies of the disturbed district were bound to unite against the insurgents.

Until the close of the eighteenth century this Covenant of Stanz formed the basis of constitutional law throughout the confederacy.

But the influence of the hermit of Obwalden proved insufficient for securing an enduring concord amid the cupidity of magistrates and the arrogance and rivalry of burghers. In various localities dissensions occurred which culminated often in open conflict, and occasionally in murder.

Hans Waldmann, the burgomaster of Zurich, and the most influential statesman of the period, inaugurated many salutary reforms, but governed with rigor, and punished with great severity all opposition to his authority. When charged by Theilig of Luzern — a hero of Giornico — with having exhibited partiality for *Insurrection in Zurich.* Austria, he caused the accuser to be seized and put to death. This summary act aroused indignation among citizens of Zurich, and strong parties antagonistic to Waldmann were quickly constituted. Affairs worked rapidly toward an open rupture within the city, and the confederates vainly endeavored to mediate. The day of insurrection arrived, and Waldmann was seized by his enemies and promptly beheaded. His last words were, "God protect thee, O Zurich, my beloved city!" A new government was inaugurated under the direction of Waldmann's antagonists, and from the unyielding severity of its rule obtained the name of the "Council of Horn." Several executions took place; the confederates again attempted to intervene; and at length, before a tribunal of allies, the city officials met the burghers, and signed an agreement known as the Convention of Wald- mann (1489). This contract secured to the people liberty to ,settle where they pleased, and to choose their own handicraft. Peasants were given the right to cultivate the land and to manage the vine according to their own judgment; and inhabitants of the country were to be entitled to share equally with city residents in the booty secured in time of war.

<small>Convention of Waldmann.</small>

At the close of the fifteenth century, Maximilian of Austria ascended the throne of Germany. The last hereditary possessions of his family in Switzerland had been lost during the reign of his father, Sigismund; and Maximilian, aware of the important advantage to be secured to the empire by a closer union with the cantons, invited the confederacy to become one of the imperial

<small>1493.</small>

circles, recognizing the imperial tribunal, and sending representatives to the imperial Diet. But the Swiss realized that their federal union was a stronger safeguard than the protection thus proffered, and declined the proposal, as well as another subsequently submitted, that they should enter the Swabian league. The discomfited Emperor designated them as refractory members of the empire, and threatened to pay them a visit, "sword in hand," but the reply of the Swiss deputies was characteristic of their nation.

"We humbly beseech your imperial majesty to dispense with such a visit, for our Swiss are rude men, and do not even respect crowns."

Opportunity seemed at hand for the execution of the imperial threat, when, in 1499, the Tyrolese undertook predatory excursions into the valley of Münster, and the inhabitants of Grisons sought aid of their Swiss allies, while their adversaries appealed to the towns of the Swabian league. The confederate response was a valiant one, and never was war carried on with more bravery. In eight months six important victories were won for Grisons, while bloody reparation for every injury to the confederacy was forced from the enemy. At Frastanz three thousand

*Swabian War.*

CLOCK TOWER AT BERN.

Austrians were left upon the field, and in the Tyrol fifteen thousand troops, attacked in their intrenchments, were completely routed by eight hundred confederates. Upon receiving intelligence of these disasters, the Emperor, who was in the Netherlands, applied for aid to the princes of his empire, and again a foreign army was marched into Grisons. The people sought the protection of their mountains, and within a few days the intruding force, overthrown by rocks hurled upon them from the heights, or buried under avalanches, was so diminished in strength, that near Dornach the survivors were easily defeated. So ended the Swabian war. In a peace negotiated at Basle (1499) the confederates obtained immunity from the jurisdiction of the imperial Chamber, and from taxes imposed by the empire. Austria made no further attempt to dissolve their league, but recognized them as practically independent, although not until 1648 was the confederacy in the eye of public law a sovereign state.[1]

*Practical Freedom from the Empire.*

Soon after the conclusion of peace-negotiations at Basle, that city was received into the confederacy. She celebrated her admission by joyful peals from

*1501. Admission of Basle.*

---
[1] See Bryce's "Holy Roman Empire."

all her chiming bells, and, displacing the guards at her gates, seated there an old woman, who, with spinning-wheel by her side, remained as an emblem of the peace and security that had descended upon the city.

Somewhat later, the desire of Schaffhausen to join the league was gratified, and in 1513 Appenzell was admitted. The confederacy then embraced thirteen members, — a number unchanged until 1798. In each of these cantons the German language was spoken, with the exception of portions of the city and canton of Freyburg.

<small>Admission of Schaffhausen and Appenzell.</small>

<small>Confederation of Thirteen States.</small>

In the original scheme of the confederation, all citizens possessed equal influence in legislation, and knight and burgher might mingle their voices in the discussions of the *Landesgemeinde*, but with the increase of population an assemblage of entire communities became impracticable, and delegates were elected by each canton to attend a Diet, or *Tagesatzung*, first assembled at Zurich. Previous to the sixteenth century, every canton enjoyed the privilege of summoning a meeting of the Diet, but that authority was subsequently vested in the *Vorort*, or directing canton, — an honor shared in rotation by Zurich, Bern,

<small>Vororte.</small>

and Luzern, except during some years succeeding the Reformation, when Catholic and Protestant cantons held separate Diets, — the former assembling at Luzern, the latter at Aargau. Deputies engaged by turn in the discussions, according to the rank of the canton they represented.

As the cantons advanced in individual strength, the sovereignty of the Diet was limited by the authority of cantonal governments, whose deputies could act only in accordance with instructions received from their states.

In time of war the influence exerted by troops was almost equal to that of a Roman army in the first centuries of the Christian era. The commands of civil magistrates were often received with the words, "A contrary decision has been formed by the vote of the army."

Torture was a common punishment for crime in the early years of the confederacy, and was considered perfectly justifiable when inflicted upon any one condemned to death. This sentence was pronounced upon all convicted of murder, blasphemy, or robbery, and at a Diet in 1480 it was decreed as the punishment for all thefts, the value of which would pay for a rope.

**Intellectual Progress.** The intellectual dimness of the middle ages had not disappeared from Switzerland in the fifteenth century; any one who could read, sing, and translate a little Latin, was considered sufficiently elevated above his associates to hold the office of pastor, and if his acquirements surpassed this limit, he was liable to be regarded as a magician. In addition to the belief in astrology and necromancy, common to the age, local superstitions were numerous. Glow-worms were indicted before the spiritual court of the Bishop of Chur, and condemned to banishment into regions uninhabited by man. One bishop issued an edict against the eels in Lake Geneva; another fulminated a similar decree against earth-worms, grasshoppers, and field-mice. If these anathemas failed to accomplish their purpose, the sins of the people were the reasons ascribed. But in 1460 the University of Basle was founded, and the German monks, who had taught that there was "a new language called Greek, the mother of all heresies, and another called Hebrew, which held the power of converting into a Jew whosoever should study it," were themselves brought to taste of the fountains of culture, opened to them through the repudiated tongues.

# CHAPTER XI

## MERCENARY SERVICE AND THE FRENCH ALLIANCE

### 1474-1516

AFTER Grandson and Morat the reputation of Swiss troops was established. The confederacy, no longer "that miniature republic, an inspiration from the glaciers and the avalanches," had developed into a nation with whom war was an instinct, and whose annals had never been stained with a military disgrace. The phrase, "God fights on the side of the Swiss!" had become proverbial, and kings vied with one another in efforts to gain the support of such puissant arms. Rivalries for this object reached the extent of governmental intrigues, and state-policy frequently deteriorated into the art of driving the best bargain for the service of troops. To secure the strongest forces, bribes were offered both secretly and openly, and freely accepted, until the mercenary motive of the confederates was so prominent that "No money, no Swiss!" became an axiom.

The hired troops were usually commanded by their own officers, and paid from the home exchequer, while the latter was reimbursed by the foreign government; but private influence was also effectual, and thousands, tempted from the cultivation of their fields by the potency of proffered gold, enlisted at so small a gratuity that it became a common saying, "The flesh of the confederates is cheaper than that of their kine."

<small>French Alliance.</small>

The system of granting pensions for the privilege of enlisting soldiers within the boundaries of the confederacy was originated by Louis XI. in 1474, and was first recorded in an appendage to the friendly compact for military service, which had been consummated twenty years earlier. Other sovereigns soon followed the example of the French king, until, in 1574, Heinrich Bullinger wrote, "It is just one hundred years since the formation of that alliance, which, as is now clear to all, was our undoing."

In 1494 Swiss troops aided Charles VIII. of France in his attempt to secure the kingdom of Naples and in the contest for Milan; although the Emperor endeavored to detach the Swiss from their French alliance, troops from the cantons were hired by Louis XII. as well as by Ludovico Sforza, and confederate fought against confederate. The home government endeavored to prevent this, but the avarice of the soldiers was dominating, and national scruples were overborne by golden arguments.

It was not strange in the universal degeneracy thus induced, that the Swiss should prove capable of treachery, and that troops hired by the Duke of Milan should desert to the King of France, bribed by his secret emissaries. When Sforza sought safety among the Swiss, and, disguised as a common soldier, joined their ranks, he was betrayed into the hands of his enemies by a native of Uri, named Rudolf Turmann. By command of the Swiss Diet, Turmann suffered death for his perfidy; but the number whose conduct had been almost equally reprehensible was so great that no adequate punishment could be inflicted.

In 1501 France and Austria were arrayed against one another, and Maximilian offered mortgages upon his estates as security to the Swiss for payment of military service; but France tempted them with ready money, and spared no efforts to win them from their allegiance to the empire. Maximilian had many partisans in Switzerland, and antagonistic feeling waxed so bitter in the cantons that a civil war seemed imminent. To avert that calamity the Diet passed resolutions in opposition to the French service; but the proffered gold exerted more potent sway, and a strong force of confederates crossed the Po, to assist the "knight" Bayard in the conquest of Genoa. When that purpose had been accomplished, they were dismissed by Louis XII., with ample pay and abundance of flattery.

The Emperor then convoked an imperial Diet at Constance, where the Swiss delegates guaranteed to provide six thousand troops for an expedition into Italy. The cantons supported the action of their deputies, but French intrigue again changed the aspect of affairs, and the disposition to support Maximilian waned. Fortunately for the peace of the country, the Italian expedition was abandoned.

When the Emperor entered the League of Cambray, which united France, Spain, Germany, and the Pope, against Venice, the suspicion, widely circulated, that the union was an overt act against all free communities, did not deter the confederates from accepting offers for their services, and six thousand aided the French army to gain

<small>League of Cambray.</small>

LAUTERBRUNNEN.

# Mercenary Service 127

the victory of Agnadello. Venice escaped destruction only through disunion among her enemies.

Pope Julius II., apprehending danger from the increasing power of France, abandoned the League of Cambray, and, in an attempt to dissolve the union of its other members, sought aid of the Swiss. The prelate Matthew Schinner, Bishop of Sion, electrified by his eloquence, while he scattered papal gold, and promised fabulous rewards, both temporal and spiritual. The Swiss, finding their services in request on all sides, demanded such exorbitant recompense that the French king broke off all negotiations with them, and the so-called "Holy League" united the confederacy with England, Spain, the Emperor, the Pope, and Venice, against France. Ten thousand Swiss, who encountered the young Gaston de Foix at the head of a French army, were hurled back upon their mountains, but when a force of twenty thousand confederates marched upon Verona the defenders of that city abandoned it to its fate. When the Swiss approached Pisa, a popular insurrection drove the French from that city, and, after a slight resistance, the troops stationed at Pavia fled across the mountains. Milan then surrendered,

*The Holy League.*

and the reinstated Maximilian Sforza rewarded the confederates with Bellinzona, Locarno, Lugano, and other districts now included in Italian Switzerland. The Pope, after conferring upon the Swiss the title of "Defenders of the Christian Church," requested that an embassy from the Diet might be sent to Rome.

Upon the death of Julius II. in 1513, Louis XII. formed an alliance with the Venetians, then estranged from their former allies, and, having bribed a band of Swiss to desert to their army, French troops again invaded Italy. Revolts in their favor opened the gates of Genoa and Milan; while Maximilian Sforza, with the Swiss in his pay, was blockaded at Novara. At that place the confederates remained faithful, although both promises and threats were profusely showered upon them by the French; and just as the garrison was reduced to the last extremity, a relief force arrived, and a complete victory over the besieging army was obtained. In compliance with imperial command, the confederates then entered France as far as Dijon, but were bribed to retreat by the unfortunate king, who had suffered recent defeat in "the battle of the Spurs."

Upon the death of Louis XII., his successor,

Francis I., desirous of recovering Milan, proposed terms of alliance with his "dear and honored friends, the Swiss." While, through the Duke of Savoy, uncle to Francis, negotiations were in progress, the French occupied Genoa, and Sforza was forced again to seek aid from those troops upon whose strength he had learned to rely. A force was despatched to join the army of Milanese, commanded by Prosper Colonna; but before assistance arrived that experienced general had been surprised and made prisoner by the French. The Swiss were on the point of turning homeward, when a chance encounter with the enemy at Marignano drew them into a battle that lasted two days. By the superior numbers of the French the Swiss were at length overborne; but the prolonged and furious conflict earned the name of "the battle of the giants"; and Francis of France exultingly stamped upon his medals, "I vanquished those whom Cæsar alone had vanquished before." 1515. Battle of the Giants.

The following year, terms of a treaty with France excluded the Swiss from Italy; but they received an indemnity of seven hundred thousand crowns, and an invitation for their nation to accept the position of godmother to the infant son of Francis I. The treaty thus consummated, and designated the "Perpetual Peace," was preserved inviolate until the overthrow of the French monarchy.

<small>The "Perpetual Peace."</small>

# CHAPTER XII

### THE "APOSTLE OF SWITZERLAND"

#### 1500-1522

THE fall of Constantinople, and the invention of printing, signalized an era that cast into Switzerland a measure of intellectual enlightenment; but the treasure was chiefly garnered by the clergy and a few among the dwellers in cities, while the mass of the people continued to exist in deepest ignorance. The clergy preferred to keep them thus, for while popular religion consisted in a tacit obedience to the commands of priests and a superstitious devotion to relics and holy symbols, the life of the prelate was an easy one, and his increasing exactions remained unchallenged.

But the notes of warning sounded by Arnold of Brescia, Huss, and Jerome of Prague had not been wholly drowned in the clash of ecclesiastical trumpets they aroused. The hour was approaching when the people would realize the necessity of reform, and freedom of conscience was a prerogative not long to be ignored in Switzerland.

Among the religious brotherhoods whose influence was dominant, the Franciscan order had obtained a pre-eminence, by means of alleged imprints of the five wounds of Christ, which were exhibited upon the body of their saint. To secure as veritable an indication of the sanctity of their own order was an ambition of the Dominican monks, and to this end, as the theatre of their operations they selected the city of Bern. There they worked upon a simple-minded tailor, named Jetzer, until they had effectually persuaded him that he was divinely called to enter their ranks. Supernatural apparitions were prepared to render him more credulous, and at length one of the brotherhood, disguised as the Virgin, drove a nail through the victim's hand, and, when a strong sleeping-draught had rendered the operations possible, produced marks upon his body which he was taught to regard as wrought by spiritual agency. He was then easily induced to act the part of a saint; and the simple people of the neighborhood heard with implicit faith the story of his ghostly visitants. But at length, during a midnight interview, Jetzer recognized a familiar voice,

*Jetzer.*

## The "Apostle of Switzerland"  133

and, suspicion being thus aroused, he soon detected the fraud that had been practised upon him. When this was known, plots were formed by the monks for putting their victim to death; but, escaping to Bern, Jetzer there entered a series of charges against the Dominican brotherhood, and the Bernese council proceeded to try all implicated in the affair, while the monks denied every accusation, and despatched delegates to mediate for them at Rome. Jetzer, tested by new tortures, was kept in confinement for months, although several Dominicans suffered death at the stake.

The scandal occasioned by these events gave impulse to the rising spirit of incredulity concerning the traditions of the Church, and hastened the approach of the Reformation, under "the Apostle of Switzerland," Ulrich Zwingli.

Zwingli — peasant, poet, scholar, patriot, reformer — had been called, when twenty-two years of age, to be parish priest in Glarus. There his influence was exerted against the enlistment of the Swiss for foreign service, although, at the summons of the Pope, he accompanied the troops of his canton in an expedition into Italy. In 1510, his poem, "The Labyrinth," represented vividly

*Ulrich Zwingli.*

to the confederates, under the figure of the Minotaur, the monster of vice, irreligion, and foreign influence that threatened to devour them.

His sojourn in Italy opened Zwingli's eyes to much that was unsound in the Church, and on his return home he began to study Greek, in order, as he said, to draw truth from the fountain-head.

One day, while visiting the priest of Mollis, Zwingli discovered a liturgy two hundred years old, in which he read these words: "After the child is baptized, let him partake of the sacrament of the Eucharist, and, likewise, of the cup." "So, then," said Zwingli, "the sacrament was at that time given in our churches under both kinds."[1] From that day his course was slow, but progressive. In 1516, called from Glarus to Einsiedeln, the sacred shrine dedicated to the Virgin, and, according to legend, consecrated by angels and apostles, he there found greater leisure for study, and devoted himself to Greek and Hebrew. The works of Origen, Ambrose, Jerome, Augustine, and Chrysostom secured his attention, not as authorities, but as counsellors, and, through much patient labor, he attained a certainty of

[1] See D'Aubigné's "History of the Reformation."

## The "Apostle of Switzerland" 135

conviction which impelled action — "attained it," writes D'Aubigné, "not like Luther, by storms that impel the soul to run hastily to a harbor of refuge, but by the peaceful influence of Scripture, whose power gradually expands the heart." When Luther's name had scarcely been heard in Switzerland, Zwingli began to preach according to his new conviction of truth. The doctrines of the exclusive agency of Christ in salvation, and of his sufficiency as a Saviour, were boldly promulgated, and the astonished pilgrims who offered candles at the shrine of the Virgin, turned homeward, marvelling at the new teachings they had heard.

In 1514 Erasmus was in Basle, and Zwingli, already familiar with the writings of "the sage of Rotterdam," was anxious to meet their author. Accordingly, a journey to Basle was undertaken, where the preacher was greeted, not by Erasmus alone, but by his friends, — Oswald Myconius, Berthold Haller, and Œcolampadius.

Contact with these scholarly minds gave Zwingli a new impulse. Oswald Myconius became his devoted friend, and, in association with other adversaries of French influence, procured Zwingli's call to Zurich. This appointment drew the

*Zwingli called to Zurich.*

reformer into a position of prominence, where he continued his practice of expounding the Scriptures to the people. On the first day of the year 1519 he preached in the cathedral of Zurich, and, after reading from the gospel of Matthew, gave so vivid and impressive an interpretation of the text that his wondering hearers exclaimed, "We never heard words like these before!"

At this period Leo X. was in the papal chair: a man of whom it has been said that "he would have been a perfect pope if he had combined with his learning, taste, and liberality, some knowledge of affairs of religion, and a greater inclination to piety." To the monk Bernard Sampson, Leo had granted authority for the sale of indulgences in Switzerland; but when, having crossed the heights of St. Gothard, the Italian friar entered the land, he encountered bold and effective antagonism. Attempting to open a market for his merchandise in the town of Bremgarten, Sampson speedily found himself opposed by Dean Bullinger, and his traffic prohibited by local ecclesiastical authority. Journeying toward Zurich, he was met by deputies who proffered the customary cup of wine to the Pope's envoy, but informed him that he might

*Bernard Sampson in Switzerland.*

be excused from entering their city. Upon receiving his declaration that he was intrusted with special messages from the Pope, the council granted him an audience, but speedily dismissed him after forcing him to remove the sentence of excommunication fulminated against Bullinger.

Leo X., whose thunderbolts of wrath were soon to be hurled against Luther, touched Zwingli with a less despotic hand, finding the Swiss nation too useful to the papal see to be lightly alienated, and Sampson was ere long recalled to Italy. Meanwhile, in other portions of Switzerland, the spirit of reform had been awakened, and new doctrines disseminated, despite the persecution that threatened its preachers. In Luzern, Oswald barely escaped death at the stake; and in Bern, Haller struggled to proclaim the Gospel in the face of many obstacles. In Zurich nearly two hundred persons confessed the faith called "Evangelical Reformed," and that city soon became the centre of the new movement.

In 1520, Zwingli was so severely attacked by the plague then raging in northern Switzerland, that his death was reported. Soon after his recovery the magistrates of Zurich forbade the clergy to preach any doctrine not drawn from the "sacred fountains of the Old and New Testament." The greater number of monks were unfamiliar with the Bible, and this decree proved the spark to kindle their long-accumulated wrath against Zwingli, who, ere long, found his life seriously threatened by their enmity.

But political complications again diverted the attention of the nation. In 1521 war broke out between Francis I. of France and the Emperor, Charles V., whose seventy-five titles provoked many jealousies in the breast of his lifelong rival. France claimed the support of the Swiss cantons, which, with the exception of Zurich, were all her allies; while the Pope, who had vibrated to the side of Charles, made an effort to secure for the empire the support of Zurich. In this purpose he was vigorously opposed by Zwingli; but the warnings of the reformer were ineffectual, and two thousand men of the city went forth to cross swords with their brother confederates. Meanwhile, **Religious Controversy.** at home, enemies were increasing around the Zurich pastor, and when, in 1522, many persons neglected to fast during Lent, the Bishop of Constance issued a mandate against reform, and sent three deputies to investigate the condition of the Church in

## The "Apostle of Switzerland"  139

Zurich. A direct blow at Zwingli was anticipated; but, in an assembly of the clergy, his learning and eloquence so effectually silenced his adversaries, that their only resource was to lay their complaints before the magistrates of the city. That body, friendly to Zwingli, recommended an appeal to the Great Council of Two Hundred, and this assembly was accordingly convened. The papal deputies endeavored to prevent the admission of Zwingli, and were at first successful; but when certain members of the council demanded that the pastors of the city should be privileged to reply to their accusers, the reformer, with his two associates, was summoned. *The Reformation in Zurich.* Again the violent attacks of the deputies were powerfully refuted by Zwingli in a calm address; and when, after a free and open discussion, the assembly dispersed, many new adherents of the Reformation had been gained.

Thus, at the same time that Luther, at Wittenberg, was maintaining the doctrine of justification by faith, Ulrich Zwingli, in Zurich, was contending for nearly *1522.* the same standpoint, — "contending," says D'Aubigné, "if less eloquently, yet with equal earnestness and honesty." Many ceremonies of the Roman Church were abandoned throughout the canton of Zurich, while, in other districts, changes of similar import were effected. The authorities endeavored to prevent extreme measures, but fanatical zeal often destroyed images, and treated even the cross with insult, while differences upon minor points of doctrine provoked frequent dissensions.

At this peroid, those who denied the efficacy of infant baptism, and insisted upon receiving the right as adults, obtained the name of *Wiedertäufer*, or Anabaptists.

## CHAPTER XIII

### THE RELIGIOUS STRUGGLE

1522–1531

INFLUENCED by papal emissaries, the general Diet that met in 1522 assumed a posture antagonistic to the Reformation, and, consequently, the council of Zurich issued variable edicts concerning religious affairs; but, after protracted deliberations, forbade any doctrines to be preached that might endanger the public peace.

Zwingli at once announced that he could not regard the prohibition, having determined to preach the Gospel freely and unconditionally; then, realizing that the hour for contesting this independent position was at hand, he convened, at Einsiedeln, a meeting of pastors who had accepted the reformed faith. In June, 1522, in the ancient chapel of the Virgin, Zwingli proposed that petitions should be sent to civil magistrates and to bishops, asking for liberty to preach the Gospel freely, and for the abolition of compulsory celibacy. The assembly were unanimous in the acceptance of tenets embodied in the petitions, and before the Diet again convened, copies of the document had been widely circulated. But, notwithstanding widespread sympathy with the principles of the reformer, secretly entertained, few persons ventured openly to espouse his cause before the Diet, and in that assembly the demands of the Zurich deputies were unsupported.

<small>Zwingli in Zurich.</small> The general vote was largely antagonistic to reform, and the Zurich petition served only as a hinge upon which revolved many future acts of hostility to Zwingli and to his cause. Oswald Myconius, who had been chiefly instrumental in circulating copies of the petition in Luzern, was forced to leave that city, and in various adjacent localities adherents of the reformer suffered serious persecution.

In January, 1523, Zwingli, resolving to meet boldly the crisis that seemed imminent, requested permission to defend his doctrines before the bishop, and, accordingly, the council of Zurich convoked a special conference in the Great Hall of the city. Before this assembly the reformer presented sixty-seven theses, in which the papal decrees and their limitations were assailed, salvation through Christ alone proclaimed, and compulsion in religious matters denounced. The similarity of his language at the close of his address, to that of the great Saxon reformer at the Diet of Worms, is noticeable. After having challenged any one present to confute the truths he had stated, Zwingli continued, "I have proclaimed that salvation is to be found in Christ alone, and it is for this that, throughout Switzerland, I am charged with being a heretic and a rebellious man. Here, then, I stand, in God's name."[1]

More than six hundred persons were gathered in the Great Hall; but at the close of Zwingli's address a silence ensued that was prolific of influence, for it was evident that no one would dispute the ground taken by so able and eloquent a champion of reform. The council then decreed that "Master Ulrich Zwingli, not being reproved by any one, might continue to preach the Gospel." Some magnates, obstinate, though embarrassed, succeeded in appointing a second conference for the following October, when, in a discussion lasting several days, the authority of the Pope, the institution of the mass, and kindred themes were freely discussed; and before a larger audience, Zwingli established the principle that fasts are optional, not obligatory, and declared the church of Zurich eman-

[1] "Nun wohlan, in dem Namen Gottes, hier bin ich."

cipated from this measure of bondage. Soon after, Zurich was detached from the jurisdiction of the Bishop of Constance, and acknowledged only the authority of civil magistrates.

The Zurich conference formed a turning-point in Zwingli's career. His adversaries realized that more vigorous measures were imperative; and while the Diet of 1524 drew up nineteen articles, which forbade preaching or conversation, in public or in private, upon the new doctrines, a papal brief induced the repudiation by Luzern, Uri, Schwyz, Unterwalden, Freyburg, and Zug, of all who endorsed the reformer's tenets. Many cities became centres of bitter controversy; the disposition of local officials toward persons suspected of favoring Zwingli grew increasingly hostile, until persecutions of the reformer's adherents often culminated in the death of the victim. But when the Pope tipped his next weapon with craft, and through his legate offered Zwingli "everything short of the papal chair," his schemes proved as powerless to bend the solid armor of steadfast purpose which enveloped the reformer, as if aimed against the everlasting hills that sentinelled the land.

In some instances the enthusiasm of converts ran into fanaticism. The Anabaptists,

ZURICH.

announcing the speedy advent of the Messiah, and the abolition of all temporal power, marked their way by deeds of horror that caused a sharp recoil from contact with the sect. One man declared himself the Messiah, another beheaded his brother as a sacrifice for the sins of the world, and only the enforcement of rigid and systematic punishment served to abate these excesses.

In various publications of this period Zwingli expounded his theological system. He maintained the possibility, through Christ's atonement, of redemption for the entire race, and claimed that the Scripture *Zwingli's Theology.* passages quoted as condemnatory of the heathen are applicable only to those who wilfully reject the Gospel. He ascribed to the sacraments a less important function than was imputed to them by the older theology, and he believed in the salvation not of baptized infants only, but of those also of heathen birth. He asserted that the virtues of the heathen are due to Divine grace, and enumerated among the saints: Socrates, the Scipios, the Catos, Seneca, Pindar, and other heroes of antiquity.

In August, 1525, the pastors of Zurich demanded from their city council in place of the celebration of the mass, the re-establishment of the Lord's Supper. A decree, in accordance with this request, was unhesitatingly issued, and signalized the year; but with the moderation characteristic of Zwingli, no other changes were immediately urged.

Meanwhile, various local governments who were in sympathy with the measures of the reformer came into frequent conflict with the Diet, and in 1526 a general conference was called at Baden for the consideration and settlement of disputed points. To Baden, a city closely allied by many interests with Rome, the council of Zurich agreed that Zwingli could not with safety go. Dr. Eck, self-assertive and assured, had volunteered as disputant upon the papal side, and Œcolampadius consented to appear as champion of the reformed faith. In a discussion, continued through eighteen days, the subjects of the real presence, the authority of the Bible, invocation of saints, adoration of images, purgatory and baptism were successively examined. By the vote taken at the close of the controversy, eighty-eight delegates adopted the theses of Eck, while Œcolampadius secured only ten adherents. Against Zwingli, denounced with every opprobrious epithet, forty charges were read, and, with all who accepted his doctrines,

*Baden Conference.*

the reformer was publicly expelled from the Catholic Church. Upon the termination of the conference the clergy of Baden celebrated triumphal services; but, notwithstanding their victory, which D'Aubigné insists was "gained by force of lungs alone," an ultimate result of the discussion was acquisition of strength by the evangelical party. Many pastors, who had hesitated in Baden to avow their convictions, upon returning to their homes exerted influence in favor of reform. Bern, after a great public disputation, declared for the new faith in 1528. Basle, the Swiss Athens, the home of Erasmus and the gentle Œcolampadius, in 1529 established the reformed church within its precincts, and Schaffhausen, St. Gall, the Graubünden, and Solothurn followed.

As the time for renewal of cantonal bonds of confederation approached, the Waldstätten declared that they could not take the oath with Zurich, and urged the exclusion of her delegates from the Diet. *Treaty of Waldshut.* The spirit of antagonism, thus stimulated, was so strongly manifested between adherents of differing faiths, that a member of either sect feared to enter a canton where the adverse belief predominated. In some districts the peasantry espoused the reformed doctrines, in anticipation of greater liberty when tithes were not claimed by monastery or abbot; but when the city whose protection was sought exacted an equal revenue, the disappointed people often abandoned their new faith, and resorted to arms in an effort to obtain exemption both from religious and secular authority.

Through the exertions of Zwingli, a defensive union was formed between Zurich, Bern, Basle, Schaffhausen, and Constance, while alliance was sought with that earnest espouser of the Protestant cause, the Landgrave of Hesse. The Waldstätten, with Freyburg and Zug, privately solicited Ferdinand of Austria to interfere on their behalf, and in 1529 concluded, at Waldshut, a treaty for that purpose. Immediately Zurich and her allies assumed a threatening attitude, while the neutral districts of Glarus, Solothurn, Appenzell, and Grisons sought to dissolve the compact of Waldshut. This effort failing, the two armies of confederates met at Kappel, where Zwingli stood among his adherents, armed for the combat. Again the neutral districts undertook the work of intervention, and through the exertions of their deputies toleration was conceded on the basis of equality of rights in religious observances, and bloodshed was temporarily prevented.

But the fire of discord was only dampened by the "*Milch-Suppe*," on the frontiers, and the flames of war soon burst forth with increased violence. Bern attempted to close her grain markets against the Waldstätten, and also refused to sell them salt or wine. With the words, "This is a hard knot, which only the sword can undo," the forest cantons declared war, and despatched eight thousand men to Kappel. Fifteen hundred Zurichers, resolute "to await the enemy in the name of God," bravely opposed the superior force. The first gun was fired by the Waldstätten, and to its summons the Zurichers responded valiantly, but the overwhelming advantage in numbers among their opponents forced even the bravest of the band to despair. Zwingli, in the forefront of battle, was stooping to console a dying man, when a stone, thrown by a Waldstätter, struck him to the ground. He rose to his feet only to receive a mortal wound, and fell backward, exclaiming, "What evil is this? They can kill the body but not the soul!" While he lay beneath a tree that now identifies the spot, a brutal soldier, recognizing him as a Zuricher by the dress, inquired if he would confess to a priest or invoke the saints, and his sign of

*Armistice of the "Milch Suppe."*

*Battle of Kappel.*

refusal was the signal for the sword-blow that closed the reformer's life. His body, recognized by his foes, was quartered and burned, and his ashes, mingled with those of swine, were scattered toward the four quarters of the earth. His heart remained unconsumed, and typified to his followers the martyr's faithful love to his country.

Had their allies acted in unison, the Zurichers might perhaps have retrieved their cause; but after the death of Zwingli nothing was achieved. A peace with the Waldstätten, signed at Deinikon, in November, 1531, established Catholicism in Solothurn, reinstated the Abbot of St. Gall, and checked the progress of the Reformation. The evangelical work begun by Zwingli was continued in Zurich by Henry Bullinger, who united different branches of the reformed church, and, through many discouraging years, with untiring energy, supported and sustained the Protestant cause. *Peace of Deinikon.*

. . . . . . . .

The differences between the teachings of Luther and Zwingli, at first apparently of minor importance, grew pronounced as their doctrines were defined with greater exactness. Luther, through the strength of his convictions upon essential truths, had been forced to renounce the authority of the papacy, but the final act had been a result of bitter struggle, while Zwingli attained gradually to the consummation of his views; through slight mental resistance, and accepted new doctrines as the results of his study of the Bible, Luther was disposed to retain in the Church all that the Bible did not expressly prohibit; Zwingli was inclined to abolish all that the Bible did not enjoin. Luther's mind was single to the propagation of truth; Zwingli was earnest in works of patriotism, and eager for civil, as well as for religious reform.

*Luther and Zwingli.*

Upon the subject of the Eucharist, the divergence in the creeds of the Reformers excited a wide controversy.[1]

The evangelist of Zurich, teaching that the sacrament is purely symbolical, and of value according to the faith that interprets it, main-

---

[1] Zwingli, in his interpretation of the meaning of the bread and wine in the sacrament, followed Carlstadt. Luther wrote in 1524, "The Carlstadt poison is spreading fast." Luther never was free of the mistake that Zwingli denied the presence of Christ in the Supper, while Zwingli distinctly says that he regards the Lord's Supper without the presence of Christ as "an enormity before which every Christian must shudder." But, according to his doctrine, Christ is not present in the lifeless bread, but in the believing soul. (From Christoffel's "Life of Zwingli.")

tained a firm opposition to the tenets of the "Wittenberg Doctor," by whom the real presence of the Saviour in the consecrated bread was strenuously claimed. Zwingli's "Commentary on True and False Religion" opened a controversy that engaged the adherents of either side, and revealed the position of many who had been keeping pace with the leaders in secret. This schism threatened disaster to the Protestant cause, and the Landgrave of Hesse, with other princes favorable to the Reformation, united in efforts to reconcile the disputants. A conference was held at Marburg in 1529, in which Œcolampadius met Luther, and Melanchthon was opposed to Zwingli, in private disputation. No ultimate ground of agreement having been attained by this means, the four stanch champions of Protestantism were confronted with one another in the presence of the Landgrave. Three days were occupied in the discussion of their tenets, but, although fourteen articles of Christian faith were accepted and signed by all, they failed to find a common basis upon which they could join hands at the Communion table.

# CHAPTER XIV

### GENEVA

#### B. C. 50 — A. D. 1526

THE largest and the richest city of Switzerland at the present day was "the farthest town of the Allobroges, and the nearest to the frontier of the Helvetii," in the time of Cæsar. Included in the Roman conquests of the first century, A. D., it passed from the grasp of the tottering empire, to become the capital of the Burgundian kingdom. Then, upon the stone gateway[1] of King Gundobald's castle, was carved the monograph that testified to a "*rex clementissimus*," and there *A.D. 433.* was wooed the King's niece, Clotilda, who, wedding the Frank, Clovis, won him, after Zülpich, to accept baptismal rites for himself and for his nation.

After somewhat more than a century of Burgundian rule, Geneva fell under the control of the Franks, and was endowed by Charlemagne with special privi- *Early Government of Geneva.*

[1] This gateway was demolished about 1836.

leges that secured the citizens against the despotism of feudal lords. Christianity is said to have been introduced in the second century by fugitives from heathen Rome, but there is no record of a bishop over the local church earlier than the year 381.

In the ninth century, the new Burgundian kingdom, evolved from ruins of Charlemagne's empire, included Geneva within its precincts; but privileges, gradually secured, by the close of the tumultuous partition period, served to render the city almost independent. Emulous of annexing it to their neighboring domain, the Counts of Savoy early attempted to encroach upon the liberties of Geneva, but the imperial protection was secured, and in 1032 the city was recognized as an appendage of the empire.

Although a nominal jurisdiction resided with the Counts of Geneva, whose castles stood on the Isle of the Rhone, the government was practically managed by four syndics, freely elected in an assembly of the people. The bishops, residing within the town, succeeded in acquiring a measure of temporal authority, and in 1124 Aymon, Count of Geneva, reserving to himself the supreme control of outlying districts, conferred, with a few restrictions, his office of vidame, or vice-regent over the city, upon the Bishop, Humbert of Grammont.

The supremacy of the Bishop as prelate and prince was recognized by the Emperor; but in the thirteenth century Savoy fomented disturbances between the ecclesiastical and secular rulers, and finally schemed to usurp the remaining rights of the latter. *Peter of Savoy.* In 1250, Peter of Savoy, surnamed "the little Charlemagne," under the pretext of securing indemnity for a debt, seized the castle of the Count of Geneva, and, by the promise of new privileges, tempted the citizens to place themselves under his protection. Although he failed to establish a permanent authority, a way was opened for further aggressions on the part of his successors.

Duke Amadeus VIII. of Savoy petitioned the Pope, "for the great advantage of the Church," to confer on him the secular authority in Geneva; but syndics, councillors, and deputies combined to resist even *Schemes of Amadeus VIII.* the papal will, in defence of their threatened liberties, and Duke Amadeus was obliged to defer the execution of his project; although he finally succeeded in effecting it through a labyrinth of manœuvres, and with the connivance of Rome.

Having abdicated the throne of Savoy to his son, he assumed the hermit's frock, but relinquished this for pontifical robes, when, under the name of Felix V., he was raised to the papacy by the Council of Basle. Upon the death of the Bishop of Geneva he made himself administrator of that diocese, which he governed by a vicar, until persuaded by the Emperor, Frederick III., to resign the papal chair. Then, transferring himself to the see of Geneva, he attained the object of his ambition, with power to transmit its prerogatives to his heirs. The dependents of these intruders encroached upon the rights of the citizens, and thronged the city, until it was asserted that more Savoyards than Genevans heard the bells of St. Peter's.

1434.

1444.

The right to appoint Bishops of Geneva, formerly monopolized by the canons of the cathedral, unless the Pope chose thus to assert his authority, was thenceforth claimed by the Dukes of Savoy; and upon the sudden death, in 1513, of Charles de Syssel, a partisan of the people against the usurpations of the reigning Duke, the suspicion was widely circulated that further encroachments upon the liberties of the city were contemplated. Influenced by the conscientious, resolute, and heroic Berthelier, the patriots resolved that successive bishops should be chosen by themselves; but Charles of Savoy succeeded in securing papal co-operation in the execution of his schemes, and Leo X. rejected the candidate freely chosen in the city. A manifesto was then issued by the Pope in favor of John, "the Bastard of Savoy," a creature wholly devoted to the interests of the Duke, whose installation into the bishopric speedily followed. His oath, in presence of the syndics, to preserve inviolate their ancient liberties, preceded by only a few hours the declaration to his courtiers, that "the next step would be to Savoyardize Geneva." The period of his tyrannical rule over the city was red with the tortures of the rack, and tumultuous through the resistance of patriots. {John of Savoy.}

The year which inaugurated the sway of the Bastard of Savoy brought also to Geneva the young Savoyard nobleman, Francis Bonnivard. His uncle, John Aimé Bonnivard, the prior of St. Victor's monastery, had bequeathed to him a small territory just without the city, over which, as prior of St. Victor's, he became sovereign prince. The young man, who had been educated in Turin, was brilliant, scholarly, liberal. Between him and Berthelier a warm friendship {Bonnivard and Berthelier.}

was soon established, and their hands joined in a compact to rescue Geneva from the power of Savoy, — a purpose to which Berthelier had consecrated his life.

Charles of Savoy found the influence of his Bishop counteracted by the diplomacy of these patriots, and in 1519, resolving upon coercive measures for the subjugation of the city, he approached the gates with a large army, and demanded free entrance. The syndics offered a welcome to the Duke and his retinue, but refused admission to the army. Characterizing them as rebellious subjects, Charles imperiously announced his determination personally to administer justice within their walls. An appeal to arms seemed inevitable, until the adherents of Savoy within the city succeeded in effecting a compromise. Upon receiving various friendly protestations from the Duke, the council consented to his entrance with a selected guard; but as soon as the gates were opened the entire army was set in motion, and the authorities of Geneva realized, too late, the danger of putting their faith in the princes of Savoy. The Savoyard army was stationed within the city, the cannon removed from the walls, and placed around the Duke's quarters, the keys of the

<small>Treachery of the Duke of Savoy.</small>

arsenal were demanded, and in a few days Geneva was prostrate at the feet of the usurper.

Previous to these events, an alliance with Freyburg and Bern had been negotiated for Geneva, through Berthelier's diplomacy, and in this extremity Besançon Hugues, a zealous patriot, contrived to escape from the city. Fleeing to Freyburg, he depicted before the council of that place the perfidy of the Duke of Savoy and Geneva's need, until, in the words of an old writer, "Every one who had anything like a heart in his breast resolved to rescue Geneva, and punish the Duke." A large force was immediately despatched to aid the imperilled city; the Duke, alarmed, agreed to retire with his troops to Savoy, and the immediate danger was averted.

*Besançon Hugues.*

At this period the appellation of Huguenots was given to the liberal party in Geneva. Previous to the Reformation, the name had a purely political significance. From the cognomen, *Eidgenossen*, or, oath-companions, by which the members of the Swiss league were known, it has been ingeniously traced through the variations Eidguenots, Eignots, and Eyguenots. It seems as reasonable to conjecture that the appellation may

*Huguenots.*

have been derived from the name of Besançon Hugues, a prominent member of the liberal league. The opposing party were characterized as Mamelukes, and compared to the Egyptian soldiers, who, having entered the service of the Sultan, relinquished their liberty, and became Mohammedans.

The Duke's entrance into Geneva had threatened serious consequences to the young prior of St. Victor's, and he was induced temporarily to desert his monastery, and to seek a refuge at Echallons, a town under the protection of Bern. Having trusted to the guidance of two perfidious nobles, Bonnivard found himself entrapped by them, and forced to sign a renunciation of his priory. He was then delivered into the hands of the Duke, by whose orders he was imprisoned in the castle of Grolée, on the banks of the Rhone, while one of his betrayers was installed at St. Victor's, and the other rewarded with a portion of the revenue pertaining to the priory.

*Bonnivard.*

Berthelier, destined to reap even more bitter fruit of patriotism, though warned of danger, refused to leave the city. Soon after the Duke's departure he was arrested by order of the Bishop, and confined in Cæsar's tower at

CASTLE OF CHILLON.

the Château de l'Île. Arrested without an accuser, he was as unrighteously tried, judged, and condemned to death, for espousing the cause of freedom.

August 23, 1519, the founder of the league, "Who touches one touches all," was executed. His head was exhibited as that of a traitor, and his property was confis- cated.  *Death of Berthelier.* After his death, the Duke of Savoy, triumphant over principles and liberties, effected various changes in the constitution of Geneva. The syndics, "more ready to lose their maces than their heads," resigned their offices, and the places were filled by adherents of the Duke. A heavy gloom overshadowed the city; the patriots, benumbed, held only rare and secret meetings; servitude and ruin seemed their inevitable doom. During three days a young girl went through the streets, refusing food or drink, and ever crying, in a monotonous and dismal voice, "Wicked Miller! Wicked Mill! Wicked Meal! All is lost! All is lost!" It seemed the farewell wail of the phantom of freedom Geneva had cherished.

But in 1520 the Duke returned to Turin, and the Bishop, having been seized with illness, left the city. Then the liberal party aroused themselves, and demanded the restoration of their franchises and the release of their imprisoned compatriots. The vicar in authority dared not resist, and the patriots, gaining courage, despatched one of their number to the Pope, with a petition that the city should be relieved from the surveillance of John of Savoy. Their request was granted; the Bastard was forbidden to return to Geneva, but, commanded to appoint his coadjutor, chose Pierre de la Baume, who entered the city the following year. Two years later John of Savoy died, suffering great agony and discerning upon the crucifix, when it was presented for his comfort, only the features of his victim, Berthelier.

<small>Banishment of "the Bastard of Savoy."</small>

Even at this early period, Geneva had evinced a tendency toward religious, as well as political enfranchisement,— through the influence, an old writer declares, of "some people called Evangelicals, who had come from France." Duke Charles of Savoy, still more exasperated by the discovery of these predilections on the part of the people, threatened to make the city "smaller than the smallest village in Savoy," but finding threats and commands equally unavailing, he resorted to artifice to establish his influence. Under the pretence of entertaining a special partiality for the city, he expressed a desire to present there his bride, Beatrice of Portugal, whose sister was soon to wed the Emperor, Charles V. The princely pair were received with honor, but the Duke's efforts proved fruitless to win a people whom he had so frequently deceived. Relinquishing the disguise of friendship, he then issued orders for the arrest of Aimé Levrier, judge of the council of Geneva, who had dared to maintain the prerogatives of the city in opposition to the demands of Savoy. Levrier was secretly seized, carried to the castle of Bonne, and, after a few days' imprisonment, was beheaded. This deed served to estrange the few friends Charles had won in Geneva, and the indignation, universally expressed, caused him to frame a hasty excuse for his departure. His arbitrary efforts to subjugate the city were nevertheless continued, until against such tyranny another appeal to the Pope was determined upon. For this purpose deputies were despatched to Rome; but, through the machinations of the Savoyards, they were stopped on their way, and detained until the influence of the Mameluke party in Geneva had again prevailed, and the city council withdrew the appeal. Charles, called "the Good," in the annals of his country, then proceeded to prepare a proscription

*[sidenote: Aimé Levrier.]*

list, which included the names of all who had opposed his capricious sway.

After the death of Levrier, the most influential citizen was Besançon Hugues, "the Nestor of Geneva," a young man, bold, devoted, and wise. He had been the chief obstacle to the progress of the Savoyard influence, and he now seemed threatened with the fate of Berthelier and Levrier.

Upon his return to Savoy, the Duke had secretly mustered another army. Silently it advanced toward Geneva, startling the patriots, who had barely time to secure the flight of their leaders. Attempting to reach the Swiss cantons, many were turned back by officers of Savoy, posted to prevent their escape. Hugues, who happened to be at his farm, a short distance out of the city, contrived to elude the traitor deputed to capture him, and reached Freyburg in safety. There he was received with honor, and in a fervid address in the council-hall he enlisted the sympathy of all present. Deputies from Freyburg accompanied the fugitives to Bern and to Solothurn, imploring the intervention of the Swiss league in behalf of Geneva; and the cantons, thus appealed to, despatched ambassadors to Savoy, declaring their determination to espouse the cause of liberty, and to oppose the unjust claims of the Duke.

Meanwhile Charles had again entered Geneva, and, availing himself of the opportunity presented by the absence of many patriots, he convened a council composed almost wholly of the Savoyard party. Even there he dared not venture save under guard of a company of archers, who, carrying their weapons high in air, gave the name of the "Council of Halberds" to the assembly. Thus supported, the Duke proclaimed his intention to spare neither money nor effort for the benefit of the city, and promised pardon to all who had opposed him, excepting only the fugitives who had sought Swiss protection. In return, he asked recognition as sovereign protector of Geneva. His address elicited applause from the assembled Mamelukes, but the adverse, and dominating influence of the city council, was revealed the day following, when the Duke's demand for the supreme jurisdiction in criminal affairs was received by the syndics with a prompt and firm refusal.

*The Council of Halberds.*

Immediately after the Council of Halberds, the Mamelukes despatched messengers to announce the result to the Swiss. The Huguenot fugitives refused to credit the humiliating statements, but when convinced of their truth, resolved to take their lives in their hands, and return to Geneva. Without safe-conduct or other protection, they hastened back, to rescue their city from the threatened servitude, or to die in the attempt.

<small>Return of the Huguenots.</small>

But already the Duke had departed for Turin, — never to return. In Geneva a reaction had occurred, the recall of the fugitives was demanded, and on a fête-day children paraded the streets, shouting, "Long live the Huguenots!" The Mamelukes, surprised and enraged, fluctuated in action. "They will go mad, please God," wrote one of the opposite party to Besançon Hugues. The Bishop, still beyond the mountains, was entreated to return, but on his arrival was greeted by a greater number of Huguenots than Mamelukes, both parties desiring to secure his co-operation. A fear that his own authority would be reduced to a minimum, should he support the decisions of the Council of Halberds, acted as the strongest influence upon La Baume's decision, and although he rejected any alliance with the Swiss, he declared, before the syndics, his approval of the fugitives, and his determination to preserve the rights of Geneva. As the time approached for the election of syndics, the resolution of the majority of citizens to reject Mameluke candidates became more and more manifest. Quietly, and without confusion, the election passed, and only when informed that four Huguenots had been appointed to rule the council did the Bishop realize how great an advance toward the freedom of the city had been attained. His command for the assembling of another general council was obeyed, but his appeal to the members there gathered failed to effect any change in their resolute purpose. Restrictions that the Duke of Savoy had enforced were annulled, and the ancient constitution, with all its franchises, was restored.

The Bishop, seeking thus his only means of safety, despatched envoys to recall the fugitives, and made extensive preparations to welcome them. A salute of guns heralded their approach, and the syndics set forth to meet them, when, accompanied by deputies from Freyburg and Bern, they triumphantly entered the city. The Council of Two Hundred convened, and received for ratification the form of alliance proposed by the Swiss. With promises of friendly intercourse, the two cantons declared themselves bound to give to Geneva "favor, aid, and succor, should

1526.

any molest her syndics, council, or freemen," and also at the city's charge to march out armies in its defence. The council testified its approbation of these terms, and the opposition offered by the Bishop was unavailing. Some conspiracies were formed, but they were detected before any serious consequences had been developed, and the partisans of Savoy soon quitted the city. On the 11th of March, eight Swiss ambassadors arrived, to receive the oath of alliance and to take it on behalf of their two cantons. This ceremony having been observed, eight citizens of Geneva were deputed to accompany the Swiss back to Freyburg and Bern to take the oath in those cities, on behalf of Geneva. The Duke made fruitless attempts to break the alliance. The Bishop, terror-stricken, sought to win favor from the Huguenots, and, conferring valuable gifts upon Besançon Hugues, despatched private envoys to Freyburg and Bern, to seek for him admission into the pivileges of their citizenship. His application was promptly rejected; but information of the overtures reached the Duke of Savoy, who, to punish this treachery, commanded the seizure of the Bishop. In a desperate attempt to save himself, La Baume ordered the arrest of the canons of Geneva, and then craved from the council permission to register his name as a freeman of the city. His protestations in favor of a liberal government gave opportunity for a request presented by the syndics for the transfer to them of all jurisdiction over civil affairs, and, having yielded this authority, the abject ecclesiastic received from the city a promise of protection. A demand from the Duke for the release of the imprisoned canons was also granted by La Baume, and twenty-four of the number sought safety in Savoy, thus freeing Geneva from the most strenuous opposers of her liberties. "God himself is conducting our affairs," said Besançon Hugues.

# CHAPTER XV

## CONFLICTS AND CONTROVERSIES

### 1527-1530

FREQUENT intercourse between Geneva and the cities of the Swiss league facilitated the dissemination of Reformed doctrines on the shores of Lake Leman. As early as 1527, Thomas ab Hofen, a friend and disciple of Zwingli, visited Geneva upon a diplomatic errand from Bern, and, filled with the missionary spirit, devoted himself, at the completion of his official duties, to the work of promulgating the tenets of the Swiss reformers. Opposed by the clergy of the city, and discouraged by the indifference of the masses, he returned to Bern without witnessing the blossoming of the seed he had planted; but the awakening of Geneva to the truth of the new doctrines were tidings spread abroad before the death of Zwingli.

Gradually opinions subversive of papal authority gained influence. The sacking of Rome by Constable Bourbon inflicted a severe shock upon the faith that had regarded papal prerogatives as divinely guarded, and proportionately strengthened the factions opposed to episcopal sway. The measures adopted by his opponents in Geneva so alarmed Pierre La Baume that he fled from the city. Freed from the surveillance of the Bishop, the citizens proceeded to reconstruct their constitution upon a liberal basis; the crest of Savoy disappeared from the Château de l'Île, and in a popular assembly the terms of a "Golden Bull" — rejecting any authority save that of Bishop and Emperor — were unanimously adopted. Threatened with excommunication, the council decreed that no mandate emanating from the papal dominion should be received, and, despite the opposition of priests and Mamelukes, and the timid apprehensions of the superstitious, a burlesque procession, "The Funeral of the Papacy," paraded the city streets.

*The "Golden Bull" of Geneva.*

These ultra demonstrations stimulated the antagonism of Savoyard nobles who resided in the vicinity of Geneva; and, having assembled at the castle of Bursinal to discuss methods of intervention, they there inaugurated the "Spoon League," with the boast that its members would "sup up the Huguenots like spoon-meat." The fraternity

*The Spoon League.*

rapidly increased in numbers. "Men took the spoon," says an old writer, "as Crusaders took the Cross," and again the independence of Geneva was seriously threatened.

The flight of his Bishop had so enraged the Duke of Savoy, that in revenge he seized upon castles belonging to La Baume, and confiscated their revenues; but, failing to advance his personal projects by this policy, he consented to a reconciliation with the Bishop, and based the new covenant upon fresh schemes for controlling Geneva. A mandate from La Baume, which forbade a trial by the magistrates alone, in any civil case, was posted upon the doors of churches; but the placards were soon removed by command of the syndics, whereupon the Bishop resorted to threats, and again the city was in wild confusion. The episcopal party, led by Hugues, declared their willingness to accept the administration of La Baume, but rejected any authority emanating from Savoy, and, in defence of their principles, stood ready to hazard their possessions and their lives.

The Sire de Pontverre, chief of the Spoon League, commanded his knights to assemble "with swords and spears," for the attack upon Geneva; but before the consummation of his schemes, in arrogant assurance of authority, he

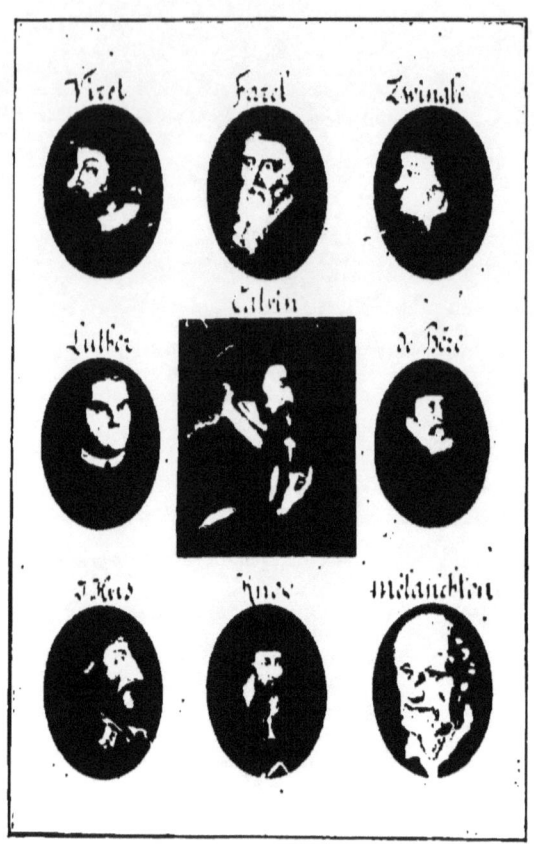

THE REFORMERS.

attempted to ride at night through the city, attended by a small escort. His insults and taunts called forth retaliatory action from the populace, and he was chased through the streets until he sought shelter in a house by the city wall, with whose occupants he was in secret league, but where he was caught by the mob and slain. Despite this disaster, the Spoon League persevered in their purpose of capturing the city, and chose a new leader for the enterprise. Everything promised a successful consummation of their plans, as amid the gloom of a moonless night the band approached Geneva, carrying long ladders with which to scale the walls. But at the moment when success seemed certain, a spirit of timidity overpowered the leaders, and, pretending to have re- ceived messages from the Duke and the Emperor, forbidding the execution of their project, they retreated as rapidly and as silently as they had advanced. "The gentlemen had undertaken to attack the city, which God has preserved hitherto," Geneva's chronicle records in its note of "The Day of the Ladders."

*The Day of the Ladders.*

Throughout this period of tumultuous political life, the Reformed religious doctrines had been steadily propagated in Geneva, through the efforts of Swiss evangelists, and the Duke of Savoy made that fact his pretext for seeking the co-operation of Pope and Emperor, in his farther efforts to humiliate and control the city. Insinuating himself into the confidence of the Swiss, he at the same time endeavored, by gifts, to gain their good-will, and by guile to sever their alliance with Geneva. The horizon of the brave city was dark with threatening clouds. Bulls of excommunication were fulminated by the Pope against all heretics, while the Emperor gave command for the arrest of any who should preach the doctrine of Reform. The reply of the Genevans to the letter containing this decree was simple and direct: —

" SIRE, — We intend to live as in past times ; according to God, and the law of Jesus Christ."

The citizens then proceeded to secure for themselves a preacher of the Evangelical faith.

Through the influence of La Baume, and of the city council, Bonnivard, after his release from imprisonment at Grolée, had recovered his priory, although its revenues remained under the control of his enemies. The friends of the new faith suggested a transfer of St. Victor's to the control of Bern, in order that under

Swiss protection an Evangelical preacher might be there established. But the Duke of Savoy coveted this stronghold so near to Geneva, and when Bonnivard, desirous of visiting his aged mother at his ancestral home of Syssel, secured a safe-conduct from the Duke, and under its protection entered Savoy, his enemies insinuated that he had gone to surrender St. Victor's. In the excitement thus engendered, threatened by the Duke's partisans on the one hand, and by the patriots of Geneva on the other, Bonnivard's return seemed so hazardous that in exchange for a pension he proposed to resign his priory to the Bishop of Montfaucon. The Bishop accepted the proposal, provided the acquiescence of Geneva and Savoy could be secured, and to consummate the matter it became necessary for Bonnivard to journey to Moudon.

At Moudon he was met by the Sire de Bellegarde, the murderer of the "father of the French Revolution," — Jacques Lefèbvre. Under the guise of an admiring friendship, Bellegarde offered every attention to Bonnivard, and when the prior announced his intention of returning to Lausanne, he insisted upon sending a servant to attend him as guide.

The proverbial saying of the Council of Con-

stance, "No faith ought to be kept with heretics," was repeated among those who
connived at the deed that followed.

*Capture of Bonnivard.*

Near Lausanne a party of horsemen appeared suddenly in the road, who demanded Bonnivard's surrender, and, despite the guarantee of safety borne by the prior, he was made prisoner, and immured in the castle of Chillon. There he was at first comfortably lodged and respectfully treated; but soon, by a special order from the Duke, he was removed to the dungeons of the castle, while the agents of Savoy in Geneva pretended ignorance of the place of his concealment.

*1530.*

Alas for Geneva! Berthelier was dead, Bonnivard in prison, the Emperor and the Pope alienated; while Charles of Savoy and Pierre La Baume, having become reconciled to one another, were concocting new schemes for her subjugation, and the Spoon League, swearing that the city should fall, stood ready to take the field at the summons of the Duke. An attack by the combined forces of the Duke, the Bishop, and the Spoon League, was projected, under the pretence of an enterprise in behalf of the "holy faith," while, as yet, in Geneva, there was not a church where mass was not celebrated. The united troops surrounded the city, but this time rescue appeared in the form of an imperial mandate, which deferred all action until spring; and, although he believed himself to be on the verge of consummating his long-cherished projects, Charles of Savoy dared not disobey the Emperor. Even while with failing hearts the citizens looked from their watch-towers, the army of the enemy was withdrawn from before their walls.

So, through repeated alarms, perils, and rescues, Geneva passed, braving assault with heroic courage, resolute in the face of intimidation, strong amid calamities, grateful for deliverances.

Intelligence of the operations of the Spoon League brought an army from Freyburg and Bern to the aid of their allies, and fifteen thousand Swiss, entering the Pays de Vaud on their way to Geneva, destroyed many castles, and desolated much property belonging to the knights of the Spoon. Upon their arrival in Geneva the large army was quartered in monasteries, where the affrighted monks were forced to provide accommodation. The Bernese, desirous of celebrating divine service according to the Evangelical forms, opened the doors of the cathedral, read the Scriptures from its pulpit, and preached there the truths of their faith, inaugurating thus a service thenceforth uninterrupted in the city.

At the end of the year, through the mediation of the allies, the truce of St. Julien was concluded between Geneva and Savoy, with reciprocal assurances of amity and good faith. Should Geneva prove recreant to her promises, the Swiss stood pledged to take up arms against her; while in case of a violation of the treaty on the part of Savoy, the Pays de Vaud would be forfeited to Freyburg and Bern.

*Truce of St. Julien.*

But the Bishop was not reinstated, and the Duke of Savoy had failed in his attempt to sever the union between Geneva and the Swiss. After the battle of Kappel, believing that he could easily extirpate heresy, Charles renewed his aggressions, and Savoyard troops again threatened the city, cutting off all its means of supply. The agents of the Duke had been active in Freyburg and Bern, and representatives of the aristocratic classes in those cities were sent to Geneva to demand the renunciation of the Swiss alliance, and the submission of the Genevans to the authority of Savoy. The citizens indignantly refused compliance with this dictate, and appealed to the Grand Council at Bern, where their deputies proclaimed their firm resolution to endure anything rather than separate from the Swiss. It was the aristocratic party alone in Bern that had been won to the interests of Savoy; the Grand Council in full assembly voted to maintain the alliance. Freyburg adopted the resolutions of Bern, and Geneva was once more in safety.

<small>1530.</small>

## CHAPTER XVI

**THE VICTORY WON**

1532–1536

FROM Orbe, Grandson, and neighboring places where they were laboring to disseminate the doctrines of the Reformed faith, William Farel, a refugee from France, and Viret, an evangelist from Vaud, watched with keenest interest the progress of affairs in Geneva. Farel, a man whom difficulties never deterred, reverses never discouraged, bold, energetic, direct in effort, entered Geneva in 1532, in company with his countryman Saunier. They were welcomed by a cousin of Calvin, Peter Robert Olivetan, who in 1530 had established himself as a tutor in Geneva. From his pen was to come the first French translation of the Bible, a work which a contemporary Waldensian synod had resolved to see accomplished.

The Huguenots assembled at once, eager to hear these "Evangelicals"; but their frequent gatherings alarmed the Catholics, and the magistrates summoned the preachers before the council. Farel produced credentials from Bern that in an assembly divided in religious opinions procured his release, but the priestly party plotted his ruin, and summoned him before the episcopal body, ostensibly for discussion of doctrine. Incited by those who had sworn that the evangelist should not escape alive, the assembly worked itself into a frenzy of antagonism, and heaped upon their prisoner insult and abuse, while refusing him any opportunity for defence. With the cry, "To the Rhone! To the Rhone! Kill him, kill him!" they struck and spat upon their helpless victim, until some of the syndics, realizing, like the official of Ephesus, that they were likely to be accused for that day's riot, opened a way of escape into the street. There the menaces of the mob were encountered, but under the protection of armed troops the evangelist escaped from the city.

The year 1533 opened tumultuously in Geneva. On the first day of January, Froment, a schoolmaster of the Reformed faith preached in the streets, by demand of the Huguenots. The day following, a proposition to forbid all preaching, either in public places, or in private houses, was brought

*Evangelists in Geneva.*

before the council. This suggestion met strong opposition, but nothing decisive followed. From Bern came complaints of the persecution of Farel and his allies, together with a demand for liberty of worship to the Huguenots. The Mameluke party resented this intervention, and united in a conspiracy for putting to death all who professed the Reformed religion. Cries of "Down with the Lutherans!" resounded through the streets. Even women bore arms, and placed hatchets and stones in the hands of their children, until for self-protection the most peaceful citizens were forced to carry weapons. The Catholics plotted a combined attack upon the Huguenots on the 28th of March. The Huguenots desired to avoid the shedding of blood, but upon learning that the destruction of their homes was threatened, they sallied forth, prepared for resistance. A bitter conflict seemed inevitable, until troops, ordered out by the syndics, dispersed the rioters. Some blood had been shed, but Freyburg's deputies in the city undertook the task of arbitration, peace-hostages were given on both sides, and a trumpet summoned the citizens to hear the herald's proclamation, "Every man shall lay down his arms, and return quietly home, without quarrel or dispute, under pain of being hanged."

*Conflicts.*

"For a time, reconciliation was the fashion," writes a chronicler of the period; and the Council of Two Hundred made attempts to frame a compromise in religious belief that might satisfy both parties. The Bible and liberty of conscience were granted on the one side, while the authority of the bishops and the observance of fast days were retained for the Catholics, and apparent harmony was temporarily restored.  But both parties were suspicious of the good faith of their former adversaries, and in May another riot was provoked, during which Pierre Wernli, a Freyburger, and a distinguished leader of the Catholic party, was killed. Freyburg demanded reparation, the Catholics gained strength, and the Pope commanded the return of the Bishop.

*Reconciliations.*

Pierre La Baume had been living at ease in Arbois, and felt no disposition to encounter the difficulties that at this juncture threatened his return to the seat of episcopal authority. But the papal will was not to be opposed with impunity, and, after obtaining from Freyburg a promise of protection, he prepared to obey. The Catholic party, believing their triumph insured, made extensive preparations for his reception, while all the Mamelukes who had left the city anticipated returning in company with the Prince-Bishop. When the subject was broached in the assembly of Two Hundred, such confusion ensued that the magistrates prohibited the admission of the exiles into the city; but, on the day appointed, eighty armed Catholics, utterly ignoring the decree of their syndics, announced their intention to form a bodyguard, and escort the Bishop home. Thus protected, La Baume entered the city, with a large company, including the chiefs of the Mameluke refugees, and magistrates from Freyburg. Hastily summoning a council, the Bishop inquired if the Genevans were prepared to recognize his authority. The stanch magistrates who replied, affirmed their determination to limit obedience to the terms of their constitution, and once again patriots and Mamelukes in the unhappy city plunged into a series of evasions, plots, and reprisals, while from Freyburg recompense for Wernli's death was demanded, and Bern strove in vain to reconcile the angry opponents. The priests, hoping to establish their personal authority, confused the people with syllogistic sophistry. "He is best fitted to be judge who is nearest God. Ecclesiastics are nearest God, therefore ecclesiastics are best fitted to judge." "As there are two

<small>Return of La Baume.</small>

great lights in the universe, so there are two in society. The Church is the sun and the State is the moon. The moon has no light of her own, all is derived from the sun. It is therefore evident that the Church possesses temporal jurisdiction over the State."

The timid Bishop felt no confidence in the fidelity of his supporters, and a few demonstrations of resistance from his opponents were sufficient to excite alarm for his personal safety. *Flight of the Bishop.* He had returned on the 1st of July, loudly proclaiming his determination to "bury the sect of Reformers." Before daylight, on the 14th of the same month, with only a few attendants, he fled secretly from the city. The citizens awoke to receive news of his departure; and the Evangelicals were jubilant, while the Catholics were in despair. By his flight the Bishop was considered to have relinquished his authority, and, ceasing to preserve for him even a semblance of respect, the citizens coined a proverb indicative of indifference: "Je ne m'en soucie pas plus que de Baume."

The priests, powerless now to prevent the circulation of the Reformed doctrines, applied to the absentee Bishop for authority to forbid preaching, and soon presented to the council the desired edict. It served, however, rather to aid than to oppress their antagonists, for the magistrates, when called upon to register a decision, ordained that "in accordance with the truth of the Scriptures, the Gospel should be preached in Geneva." When, to strengthen the Catholic influence, a Dominican priest, named Furbity, was appointed to conduct service in the cathedral, and the Evangelicals were challenged to dispute with him, the influence of Bern sent William Farel again to the city. The right to hear their preacher from their cathedral desk was claimed by the Reformed party, but to prevent so great a desecration of the sanctuary, the Catholics declared themselves ready to risk their lives. At this junc-

*Bern supports Farel.* ture, Baudichon de la Maisonneuve, an influential and diplomatic citizen of Geneva, presented to the council a letter from Bern, which demanded that a pulpit be provided for Farel, and threatened the prosecution of Furbity for his attacks upon a man under Bernese protection. Soon a Bernese embassy arrived, bringing another supporter of the Reformed faith, — the young and modest Viret, — destined to prove a formidable adversary to the Catholics.

Meanwhile the Bishop of Geneva watched the

LAKE OF GENEVA.

progress of affairs from afar, and, too timid to trust himself in the vicinity of the city, yet unwilling to relinquish his semblance of power, he signed at Arbois a document which gave authority to a lieutenant to execute law in his name.  A new scheme was concocted by the crafty ecclesiastic, in conjunction with the Freyburg council, the Duke of Savoy, and the Mameluke party; but the accidental capture by the patriots of some private papers belonging to La Baume rendered these projects abortive. The documents revealed the Bishop as an instigator of discord in Geneva, and convinced the syndics that to secure themselves against his intrigues the most ultra measures were necessary.  Then in the Great Council of the "White City of the Lake" a resolution was deliberately and solemnly adopted to renounce, thenceforth, the authority of a bishop, and to be governed only by magistrates favorable to the Reformation and to the Swiss alliance.

*Authority of the Bishop renounced.*

Still the churches were claimed for the old worship, and, failing to find another place large enough to accommodate the crowds who gathered to listen to Farel, de la Maisonneuve led the Huguenots to Rive, and, taking possession of the convent and court, informed the scandalized monks that Farel would preach there. Service was publicly announced by the ringing of the convent bells, and a motley assembly, embracing priests and monks, as well as Huguenots, gathered to listen to the ardent and earnest preacher, whose influence from that day extended over many of the priestly class. Some advocates of the new doctrines, impelled to a fanatical zeal, destroyed images in the Franciscan cloister, but the syndics of Geneva quickly enforced order, and imprisoned the iconoclasts.

Instigated by Catholic princes and prelates, and influenced by the Emperor's wish for the **Destruction of St. Victor's.** reinstallation of the Bishop, the Duke of Savoy sought to force from the Genevans a recantation of the doctrines they had accepted, and ere long castles in the city's vicinity were garrisoned by Savoyards, while at Luzern a Swiss assembly consented to the Duke's demand for the return of La Baume. While from Gex, where he had located himself in safety, the Bishop hurled bolts of excommunication against his recreant subjects, Geneva received the bitter tidings that Bern had deserted her. But the resolute citizens declared their determination sooner to set fire to the four corners of their town than surrender their right to freedom of worship, and, more securely to fortify themselves against assault, they demolished many strong places in their suburbs.[1]

Still undismayed, although in extreme peril of their lives, Farel, Viret, and the evangelist Froment, pursued their work. In a public theological discussion, a victory was won by the Reformers, which silenced the champions of the Pope and procured the abolition of the Mass. The Duke of Savoy pronounced Geneva plague-stricken, and in obstinate pursuit of victory again appealed for Bernese aid; but, weary of the long struggle, Bern declined again to participate, unless as mediator. A little band from Neuchâtel, roused to sympathy for Geneva, ventured to her relief under the command of Jacques Baillod, surnamed, from his courageous temperament, "Wildermuth." Near Gingins they defeated a force belonging to the knights of the Spoon; but before any actual relief for the beleaguered city had been secured, Bernese deputies persuaded Wildermuth to retire, and with strategies and reprisals the conflict continued.

A change of policy on the part of Bern was at last induced by the ambitious projects of the

---

[1] The first walls destroyed were those of St. Victor's: The priory had been founded in the sixth century by Queen Sedelenba, sister to Clotilda, in memory of the victories of Clovis.

King of France. Francis I., desirous of possessing Milan, regarded Savoy as a profitable preliminary acquisition, and, with the ultimate aim of provoking a war with the Duke, he despatched a body of troops to the relief of Geneva. Bern, jealous of French influence on territory that she coveted, immediately declared war against Savoy, on the pretext of violations of the treaty of St. Julien; and, marching an army into the district of Vaud, the Bernese set fire to Savoyard fortresses, and desolated the land. Geneva was speedily relieved from the environment of the Spoon League, and the entire Pays de Vaud passed into the possession of Bern. On the 27th of March, Chillon was captured by an army of combined Bernese and Genevese troops. When, having sought out the dungeon of the prior of St. Victor's, the liberators shouted, "Bonnivard, you are free!" the captive's response echoed along the vaulted archways, "Et Genève?" Triumphantly the answering shout was repeated, "Geneva also is free!" and Bonnivard came forth to find the city he had left under papal sway and subject to Savoyard tyranny, a free republic, strong in the Evangelical faith.

An unanticipated danger was presented in the attempt made by the lords of Bern to claim the prerogatives of former bishops in the city, but the threatened feud ended in an amicable agreement of co-burghership between "the free towns of Bern and Geneva."   *1535.*

Meanwhile a French army had invaded Savoy, and Charles III., abandoned by the Emperor, and robbed of his possessions, ended his life, at the close of the year, in dejection and misery.  His son, Emanuel Philibert, succeeded in recovering his inheritance from the French, but left Geneva unmolested.   *1535.*

On the 27th of May, 1536, the bell of St. Peter's again summoned the citizens to assemble within the cathedral walls.  With unanimity, unbroken by a dissenting voice, an oath was solemnly taken, "to abolish the mass, images, idols, and other papal abuses," and to live "according to the Word of God, as it is daily preached."  *The Establishment of the Reformed Religion.*

# CHAPTER XVII

### CALVIN IN GENEVA

### 1536–1564

FROM the tottering republic of Geneva, neither political nor religious anarchy could be immediately banished, although the council legalized the new form of worship, and decreed the administration three times a year of the sacrament of the Lord's Supper. When the same authority abolished all festival days except Sunday, and forbade all worldly entertainments, restraints were imposed, against which a large number of the citizens rebelled, and the stentorian voice of Farel inveighed ineffectually against indulgence in prohibited recreations.

The zealous, resolute, and fearless evangelist was struggling against antagonistic influences that threatened to overpower him, when, in August, 1536, Calvin arrived in Geneva. A fugitive from his native France, on account of his advocacy of ecclesiastical reform, Calvin, during two years, had been a

*Calvin.*

wanderer. At Strassburg he had published the first Latin edition of his "Institutes of the Christian Religion," — a work styled, by his enemies, "the Koran of the Heretics." In the spring of the same year he visited the court of Ferrara, where the good Duchess Renée welcomed all who were in sympathy with the new religion. Returning thence to Strassburg, with the intention of remaining in that city for a period of quiet study, Calvin rested over-night in Geneva. News of his arrival having been carried to Farel, the evangelist at once determined to secure the assistance of his fellow-countryman in the toilsome task of reforming the pleasure-loving city of the Lake. With characteristic vehement eloquence he pleaded for assistance, while Calvin, protesting unfitness for the duty and desire for study, resolutely refused to listen to his importunities. At length, the inflexible Farel declared that the curse of God would rest upon his compatriot if he persisted in his refusal, and so vehemently urged the claims of his work that Calvin declared he felt as if the hand of the Almighty had been stretched out from Heaven and laid upon him.

The promise to remain was gained, but for a while Calvin seems to have worked almost incognito in Geneva. A decree of the council is recorded, showing that, in response to a request from Farel, "six écus[1] and a cloth coat" were bestowed upon "that Frenchman recently arrived," whose lectures were declared upon the authority of his co-laborer to be "very necessary to the welfare of the city." Public attention was directed toward the preacher by his eloquent utterances in an important disputation at Lausanne, which, in September, 1536, he attended in company with Farel. Upon his return his instructive extemporaneous lectures at St. Peter's were continued, and a catechism, which he formulated, was sanctioned by the council, in conjunction with a confession of faith drawn up by Farel. Regulations for the conduct of daily life were at this time publicly promulgated, and any violation of their restrictions was punished by the magistrates.

The following laws are recorded: —

"Violators of the Sabbath shall receive public admonition from the pulpit."

"The gamester shall be exposed in the pillory, with a pack of cards tied around his neck."

"A dinner for ten persons shall consist of no more than five dishes."

[1] About eighteen francs.

CATHEDRAL ST. PETER, GENEVA.

On the 20th of May, 1537, the records show that a bride who had walked out on the preceding Sunday, with her hair curled to an extent deemed unseemly, was sentenced to imprisonment, together with her companions and the hairdresser whose art had been thus exhibited.

Such limitations, in minor matters of conduct, provoked a fierce opposition from the liberal party in Geneva, who were known as "Libertines," and the discord was increased when the council made the acceptance of the Evangelical confession of faith obligatory upon every citizen. November 12, was appointed for those who had not already taken the oath of assent to assemble in the cathedral for that purpose, and whoever refused to comply was sentenced to banishment. Calvin had insisted upon his authority to exclude from the sacrament of the Lord's Supper any whom he deemed unworthy to partake, and disputes upon this point threatened anarchy. The Bernese blamed the council for the disorder, and at length the syndics decreed that the sacrament should not be refused to any one.[1] At the next election, the magistrates chosen were all antagonistic to the Reformation, and Calvin was soon

[1] See "Registers of Geneva," January 3 and 4, 1538.

seriously fettered in his work, while, throughout the city, disorders prevailed to such an extent that the evangelists informed the council that it would be "impossible to administer the sacrament in the midst of such profligacies and blasphemies." Thereupon Calvin, Farel, and Viret were alike forbidden to hold any religious services; but, despite the injunction, each entered his pulpit at the customary hour on Easter Sunday. Motley crowds, including both adversaries and friends, attended, and at the evening service, in Calvin's church, the excitement reached such a crisis that swords were drawn, and bloodshed was with difficulty prevented, while the escort of a guard was necessary to attend the preacher home.

*Riots.*

*Banishment of the Evangelists.*

The following day the proposition of the syndics, to imprison the ministers for violation of magisterial ordinances, was changed by the council to sentences of banishment. Calvin went to Strassburg, where he entered upon the charge of a church of French refugees, while Farel was warmly welcomed at Neuchâtel, and Viret became pastor at Lausanne. Bernese envoys to Geneva remonstrated against the expulsion of the preachers, but the Libertine party swayed the council, and no repeal of the decree could be obtained. Many institutions opposed by the evangelists were soon re-established; and so strong was the reaction in the city, that the Bishop even cherished a hope of reinstalment. The Pope solicited the aid of neighboring ecclesiastics in the work of proselytizing anew the Genevese, and a letter was written, inviting them to return to the bosom of the Church. This document, prepared by a French bishop, named Sadoleto, was received by the council on the 26th of March, 1539. They were in deliberation upon a reply, when an address sent to Sadoleto by Calvin was made public, and produced everywhere a profound impression.

Calvin had read, at Strassburg, the letter of Sadoleto to the Genevese; and at the suggestion of his Strassburg friends, "apprehending what evil it might bring to Geneva," he undertook the task of composing a reply. His letter, said Luther, "had hands and feet," and struck an effective blow at the Catholic party. Published in Geneva, it induced a strong reaction in favor of the banished preacher. Already the political clique that had exiled the evangelists was divided; the leaders of the Libertine party, having become offensive to their partisans, had

*Calvin's Letter to Sadoleto.*

been in their turn banished; and the distracting condition of the city, where disorders were rapidly increasing, caused the magistrates to repent the expulsion of the pastors. The citizens united with the council in an urgent call for Calvin's return, and in 1541, reluctantly yielding to the repeated summons, the preacher re-entered the city, was installed in a house near the cathedral, and decreed an annual salary of five hundred florins, twelve measures of wheat, and two tubs of wine.

*Calvin's Recall.*

While in Strassburg he had married Idelette de Buren, "a grave and pious widow," whose first husband he had converted from the Anabaptist belief.

Calvin returned to Geneva, he states, "with sadness, tears, anxiety, and distress of mind, at taking again so great a burden." The number of Libertines in the city was still sufficient to form a dangerous faction, and in sympathy with them upon many points was another party, who called themselves Patriots. To deter the reformer from the prosecution of his work, various acts of insubordination were attempted. Shots were fired in the night at his door. He was set upon by dogs, and his clothing and flesh torn. But unflinchingly and without vindictiveness he pursued his way, and under his controlling influence both the civil and the ecclesiastical laws of the "Protestant Rome" were reformulated upon the basis of a co-operative union of Church and State. The city councils retained their prerogatives, but ecclesiastical discipline was vested in the hands of six preachers and twelve laymen, who formed the Consistory. This body also exercised a general moral supervision over the citizens, and held the power of excommunication, with that of transferring to the magistrates, for discipline, all criminals deemed by them guilty of penal offences.

By the stern code of laws then adopted, death by fire was the penalty of heresy. All dancing and card-playing were forbidden. To give the name of a Catholic saint to a child was a penal offence; drunkenness and blasphemy were punished with severity, and in 1568 a child was beheaded for striking its parents, while another, for attempting the same offence, was whipped through the streets, and banished from the city.

The ministers, who were known as the "Venerable Company," met once a week for "mutual fraternal censure." A school was established which received pupils from Basle,

Bern, and even from Zurich. Instruction was given in "the three most excellent languages, Greek, Hebrew, and Latin," as well as in French, and lessons began at five o'clock in the morning. Geneva, "the theological city," became an asylum for religious refugees, while from thirty-four printing-presses the Reformed doctrines were scattered abroad.[1] Here Calvin continued to labor uninterruptedly for twenty-three years, preaching and teaching, writing theological treatises, and corresponding with theologians, nobles, and princes, attending the meetings of the Consistory and of the Senate, entertaining strangers, and counselling all who appealed to him for advice. The biographers, who censure most severely his bigotry and the harshness of his judgments, admit the purity of his motives, and his unswerving fidelity to duty. His personal humility and his strictness in self-discipline were prominent traits, often overlooked in the contemplation of his austerity and censoriousness. He has been compared to a Roman censor, and to a Hebrew prophet,[2] while despotic treatment of all who

[1] The so-called "five points of Calvinism" are: Unconditional election, limited atonement, the impotency of the human will, irresistible grace, and the perseverance of all believers.

[2] Review of German authors on Calvin by Dr. Schaff in "Princeton Review," April, 1875.

differed from him in religious opinion is ascribed to his strong conviction of the responsibility of rulers for the extermination of heresy; a principle universally accepted, previous to the seventeenth century.[1]

A conspicuous instance of Calvin's unyielding severity was shown in the doom decreed to the Spanish theologian, Michael Servetus, whose denial of the doctrine of the Trinity had placed him in antagonism to both Catholics and Protestants. In a correspondence with Calvin, Servetus did not hesitate to attack the Christian creed, and in his books, "Errors of the Trinity," and "The Restoration of Christianity," he gave publicity to sentiments so obnoxious that difficulty was experienced in getting the latter work printed. Arrested in Lyons, Servetus was carried before an ecclesiastical court, but contrived to escape that surveillance, and was on his way to Italy, where he anticipated less opposition, when, by Calvin's command, he was arrested in Geneva.

*Servetus.*

It has been asserted that Calvin believed he would be able to force from his adversary a recantation of his published dogmas, and that the Reformer did not anticipate the fatal result of the arrest he commanded, although personal

[1] See Fisher's "History of the Reformation."

antipathies were doubtless united to doctrinal differences between the controversialists. After the imprisonment of Servetus, Calvin wrote to Farel: "I hope the sentence will be capital, but desire the atrocity of the punishment to be abated."[1]

But Servetus steadfastly refused to retract or to modify any of his doctrines, and boldly demanded Calvin's punishment for malicious prosecution. Contrary to his expectation, his claims failed to receive consideration from the council, who condemned him to die at the stake on the 27th of October, 1553.

At this period Calvin had many political adversaries in Geneva. At the head of the Libertine party stood a son of the patriot Berthelier, to whom the Reformer had recently refused the sacrament. A conflict with Berthelier's adherents ensued, when they attempted to supplant the authority of the Consistory by that of the Senate; but their efforts, though culminating in armed insurrection, were soon overpowered, Berthelier was executed, and the Libertine party was rendered impotent for further manœuvres.

Geneva was at last free from faction; and, although called by the Pope "a nest of devils

---

[1] See Dyer's "Life of Calvin."

and apostates," the industrious and Christian republic became "the hearthstone of Protestantism," the city of which John Knox wrote: "Elsewhere the word of God is taught as purely, but never, anywhere, have I seen God obeyed as faithfully."

In this fair city of his adoption, at the close of a day in May, 1564, Calvin died, worn out with labor and anxiety, although not quite forty-five years of age. The republic mourned for the preacher who had served it with undeviating conscientious faithfulness, but his commands forbade them to mark his grave by any monument in the cemetery of Plainpalais. The traveller seeks in vain for the resting-place of the Reformer, who has been called by a modern sceptic "the most Christian man of his generation."

# CHAPTER XVIII

## THE BORROMEAN LEAGUE

### 1555-1641

IN Locarno, and other Italian districts over which Swiss authority had been extended, the Unitarian doctrines, promulgated by Socinius, gained many adherents; but ere long the installation of Catholic bailiffs drove into exile all who had openly embraced the new faith. In **Emigrants from Italy.** 1555 one hundred and fifty Italian families emigrated to the north of the Alps, carrying with them the Southern art of silk-weaving.

A powerful coalition against Protestantism was formed in Europe soon after the accession to the throne of Spain of the gloomy and bigoted Philip II., and, fortified by the new orders of Jesuits and Capuchins, the coadjutants extended their influence into Switzerland. In 1564, profiting by the stimulated antipathy to Reform, Emanuel Philibert of Savoy demanded of the Swiss the restitution of lands conquered by them in 1536, and Bern was forced reluctantly to relinquish a portion of territory. In the region restored to him, the Duke installed a company of Jesuits under the guidance of the gentle and strong François de Sales, and through the instrumentality of this "Bishop of Geneva" Catholicism was re-established in a portion of the district recently evangelized.

Meanwhile, Cardinal Charles Borromeo, the zealous Archbishop of Milan, journeyed on foot through Switzerland, laboring to unite the members of the confederacy in a league pledged to support Catholicism, and to wage a holy war against the Protestants, while other emissaries of the Pope exerted themselves to sow throughout the cantons seeds of civil discord, in order thus to arrest the spread of the Reformation. Antagonisms thus excited waxed so bitter between adherents of differing faiths that in 1582 the Protestants refused to receive the new calendar of Pope Gregory XIII. *Influence of Charles Borromeo.*

In 1580 Borromeo succeeded in establishing a papal nuncio in Luzern, and in 1586 the oath of the Borromean or Golden League was taken by seven cantons,— the four Waldstätten, Zug, Freyburg, *The Borromean League.*

and Solothurn.[1] By one of its articles this compact was pronounced superior in authority to the original *Bundesbrief* of the confederacy. It bound the cantons to take up arms against any in their midst who should tolerate the doctrines of the Reformed religion, and a necessary sequence of its acceptance was the severance of ties with all who had embraced Protestantism. The incorporation of the Borromean league marked the final division of the cantons into two antagonistic religious parties.

In 1557, the desire of Geneva to enter the Helvetic league met refusal, owing to a Catholic majority in the Diet; and the adverse vote was emphasized by Louis Pfyffer, the avoyer of Luzern, and a dominating spirit among the Catholics, who publicly expressed a wish for the very extermination of the city of Calvin. Emanuel Philibert of Savoy, becoming cognizant of the antagonistic disposition fostered throughout Catholic Switzerland toward Geneva, projected fresh schemes for the conquest of the city; but, baffled in these, turned toward the Pays de Vaud, and marched an army against Lausanne. There the burgomaster, Isbrand d'Aux, a pensioner of Savoy,

*Savoyard Ambition.*

---

[1] These cantons with Valais and Ticino form the present Catholic Switzerland.

stood ready to deliver everything into his hands; but the traitorous designs were revealed by a Vaudois, named David de Cronsaz, and evoked from Bern a declaration of war against the Duke. The commander of the Bernese army, Jean de Wattenwyl, was secretly in league with Savoy, and when his transactions were exposed the indignant citizens of Bern forced him into exile. But as city-avoyer, his sentiments had influenced the senate of Bern in large measure, and Geneva must have remained subject to Savoyard aggressions, had it not received the support of the French king. Henry of Navarre volunteered to protect the city, and in 1598, by the treaty of Vervins, France received, in compensation for this service, the district of Gex.

A final attempt to grasp Geneva was made in 1602, when the reigning Duke, Charles Emanuel of Savoy, deemed the opportunity for success at hand, and on a dark December night approached the unsuspicious city. Incited by words from the Jesuit priests, "Mount courageously; every round of the ladder is a step toward Heaven," the Savoyard soldiers scaled the walls without alarming the sentinels. The citizens, awakened by outcries in the streets, found several hundreds of the enemy already within their gates, but, defending themselves with intrepid bravery, they repulsed the invaders, and took captive thirteen nobles of Savoy, who, after the Duke and his army had been forced to retire, were speedily put to death.

This audacious exploit of the "Escalade" roused Protestant Europe against the Duke of Savoy. His embassy to Bern, sent with excuses for infringement of the treaty with that canton, was received with disrespect, and a general war then threatened was averted only by the instrumentality of France, Spain, and the Pope. At St. Julien, July 21, 1603, the terms of a peace were dictated, which prohibited the advance of Savoyard troops within sixteen miles of Geneva.

*The "Escalade."*

*Peace of St. Julien.*

. . . . . . . .

Again was Switzerland doomed to be desolated by disasters. A plague visited Basle in 1610, sweeping away nearly four thousand inhabitants, and the year following nearly a quarter of the entire population of the interior were destroyed by a similar scourge. In 1618 the rich town of Pleurs, in the Chiavenna, was buried beneath a landslide, and twenty-five hundred lives were lost. But these calamities failed to divert

*Disasters.*

ST. GOTTHARD PASS.

## The Borromean League 209

the survivors from their civil conflicts, and a new apple of discord between the Swiss and the Hapsburgers was fast ripening.

After the victory of Pavia (1525) had secured to Spain all Lombardy, the district of the Valtelina[1] was coveted by the Spanish king as affording the most direct route between the Tyrol and Milan. France, watching with jealous eyes every effort of her formidable rival for the acquisition of territory, warned the Grisons of designs to despoil them. Many lords of the region had been bribed to partisanship, and cliques, led by members of the two most influential families in the country, Planta and Salis, espoused respectively the Spanish and the French interests, while the faction of Travers worked for the Venetians, and the national party refused any foreign alliance or influence. Between the years 1574 and 1665 civil war raged in the Grisons, and the intervention of the confederates secured only a temporary calm. A free Rhetia was to be the Phœnix born of many desolated villages. *Divisions in the Grisons. Planta and Salis.*

A crisis of excitement occurred when the communes established a criminal court at Chur,

[1] The Valtelina was acquired by the Swiss after the battle of Marignano.

for trial of all who were suspected of an influence prejudicial to the interests of the country. Innocent as well as guilty were proscribed, and religious differences fanned the flames of political opposition. A report that the Viceroy of Milan meditated a massacre of Protestants moved the people to such a frenzy that Planta was forced to fly, and the Reformed party, temporarily triumphant, banished or put to death many of the opposite faith. The exiled persons conspired with the Hapsburgs for an invasion of their country and the extirpation of the Protestant religion. The brothers Planta were leaders of a band who, in 1620, attacked villages in the Valtelina, perpetrated frightful barbarities, and ruthlessly murdered men, women, and children. Six hundred persons are estimated to have perished in this so-called "St. Bartholomew of the Grisons." Two thousand Bernese and one thousand Zurichers marched to the rescue of their brethren in the faith, but suffered defeat in a bloody battle (September, 1620). The Gray League, Catholic in its preferences, declined to render aid, and, animated by the suggestions of Pompey Planta, discussed the project of a separation from the union of the Grisons, and an alliance with the Waldstätten. Their

*The St. Bartholomew of the Grisons.*

schemes were opposed by Jenatsch, a Protestant pastor in command of troops belonging to the national party. By adherents of this faction Planta was assassinated, at his château of Rielberg, the Catholics were soon afterward defeated in a battle near Varendas, and Jenatsch was master of the Valtelina.

Then Austria, declaring, "Since you wish for war, you shall have war," ordered her troops into the Grisons, and the unhappy land suffered such chastisement as had been endured by the Waldstätten in the days of their subjugation to the arbitrary bailiffs of Austria. The peasantry were treated like cattle, and driven before the lash, while Balderon, commander of the invading forces, perpetrated so many atrocities that he obtained the name of "the new Holofernes." The Reformed clergy were summarily ejected from their pulpits, and seventy-five churches became pastorless; but when an attempt to compel attendance at Mass was made, the limit of submission was passed. "If we must lose our liberty, let us save our souls!" was the cry of the helpless peasants, as they fled from their persecutors into the woods. The men of Prettigau attempted resistance, and, having armed themselves with sticks and clubs,

*Austrian Incursions.*

*Balderon.*

surprised an Austrian garrison on Palm Sunday, 1622, killed four hundred, and drove the remnant from the land. But Balderon returned with ten thousand troops, and again there were massacres and battles in the valleys and upon the mountains. A little band of thirty patriots, with heroism worthy of the men of Thermopylæ, faced the crowded Austrian ranks in a bitter battle, and fell there, one by one. Attempted intercession for the unfortunate people, by the confederates, proved unavailing; the Austrian grasp was strong and unyielding. At length France interfered, and, veiling secret designs under the guise of a protective friendship, sent into the Grisons an army under command of "the good Duc de Rohan." By this assistance Austria's troops were driven from the district, and the Valtelina, that "Helen of a new Trojan war," was ransomed. **French Interference.** But the crafty Duke who guided the helm of France had projected further achievements, and too late the people of the Grisons perceived that they had only changed masters.

Then, in a secret gathering at Chur, the patriots, with Jenatsch at their head, took a solemn oath to liberate their land, and three months later, rising as one man, the people of the Grisons expelled the French. Ambassadors were then despatched to the courts of France, Spain, and Austria, and while the burden of the "Thirty Years' War" was pressing heavily upon the nations they entered readily into peaceful negotiations with Grisons. Soon afterward the district included in the league of the Ten Jurisdictions purchased the remaining rights of Austria in that territory, and when the lower Engadine had obtained equal immunities the Hapsburgs remained in possession of but a few insignificant prerogatives, and the Grisons called itself free. This independence was in 1641 formally recognized by Austria, France, and Spain, in the treaties of Milan and Feldkirch.

*Freedom of the Grisons.*

## CHAPTER XIX

### FREEDOM FROM THE EMPIRE

#### 1618–1712

DURING the period covered by the "Thirty Years' War" the aid of the Swiss was solicited both openly and privately by Protestants and by Catholics; but every temptation to engage in the conflict was opposed by the Diet, and, with the exception of a few unforeseen complications, a strict neutrality was preserved.

*The Thirty Years' War.*

In one or two places, where the guaranteed neutrality had been ignored by subordinate local officials, temporary disturbances occurred. A garrison of Zurichers, who guarded the frontier at Stein, in Thurgau, allowed the Swedish army to pass on its way to Constance. The Austrians speedily imitated the example of the Swedes, and traversed Swiss territory *en route* to the city of Rheinfelden. The canton of Schaffhausen and the bishopric of Basle suffered seriously from the inroads of the

Swedes, who, in their greed for plunder, often suspended the unhappy peasants by their feet, upon their own hearthstones, in the hope of forcing from them a renunciation of the wealth they were suspected to possess.

A spirit of universal suspicion was awakened by these depredations, and between Protestant and Catholic cantons accusations of treason were freely interchanged. One side threatened to send reinforcements to the Swedish army if the other evinced partiality for the Austrians, and the jealous dissensions ceased only with the termination of the war.

While peace negotiations were in progress at Westphalia, the confederates despatched to the council a firm and wise ambassador, Rudolf Wettstein, burgomaster of Basle, through whose skilful diplomacy, aided by the French envoy, Henri de Longueville, a formal imperial acknowledgment of the independence and self-sovereignty of the Swiss was obtained. *The Peace of Westphalia.* *1648.* No longer the Emperor's mandates were addressed to "Subjects, beloved and faithful to ourselves and to the empire," but by the epithets, "strong, steadfast, honored, and especially dear," the position of the Swiss nation was recognized.

The kingdoms of Europe offered honorable fellowship, and with the music of trumpets and drums the imperial message was promulgated in cities, while in every village of the confederacy the declaration of independence was publicly read, amid rejoicings only paralleled in the heroic days of Morgarten and Sempach.

. . . . . . . .

Although the principles of democracy had exerted controlling authority in the formation of many Swiss institutions, the spirit of the community had not been penetrated to the entire exclusion of aristocratic sovereignty, and in many portions of the land the peasantry were no better off than when their government had been more absolute in form. After the Peace of Westphalia had established the confederacy upon its firm basis of national freedom, the peasants in the larger cantons, having borne willing part in the wars for independence, believed themselves entitled to the privileges long possessed by the men of the Waldstätten, and, in conjunction with some less legitimate prerogative, they demanded the right to elect their own magistrates. As the towns had sought freedom from the rule of counts and seignors, the peasants throughout the country now sought emancipa-

<small>The Peasants' Revolt.</small>

## Freedom from the Empire 217

tion from the rule of the towns, and complaints were frequent of heavy taxes imposed by city officials. Upon the promulgation of a government ordinance which depreciated the value of the currency and rejected agricultural products in payment of taxes, the widespread discontent ripened into resistance. Three men from the town of Entlibuch assumed the antique costume of the men of Rütli, and, followed by companions sounding Alpine horns, led a multitude to the town of Dorf, where deputies from the cities were in session. A demand for decreased taxes, increased interest upon loaned money, and other concessions to the populace, was presented to the council through the banneret Emmenegger, and then, in company with malcontents from ten bailiwicks, the Entlibuchers joined at Wollhausen in a solemn league to maintain all the rights thus claimed, and to meet opposing decrees with armed resistance.

The spirit of rebellion thus manifested rapidly spread, and when the magistrates of Bern summoned their peasantry to arm for the protection of the confederacy, refusals to march against their fellow-sufferers and complaints of individual wrongs to be redressed were the response to the call. The united troops of the thirteen cantons were then demanded by the Vorort, but at the suggestion of Zurich and Luzern arbitration was attempted. While deliberations were pending, the peasantry of Bern were excited by the entrance upon their territory of some troops from Schaffhausen, who had been despatched in immediate response to the call of the Vorort, and a general rising followed, in which the castles of the land-vogts were assaulted, and numerous acts of violence committed, while through the French ambassador the peasants solicited foreign aid.

These overtures were quickly betrayed to the Bernese government, and many persons who had been in sympathy with the insurgents while their fidelity to their land remained unimpeachable, became opponents of their course when aware that French interference had been sought.

At length the deputies assembled at Bern succeeded in effecting a compromise between the prerogatives claimed by the magistrates, and the demands made by the communes, and, according to a prescribed programme, delegates from the revolted districts asked pardon of the city council for acts of insubordination. When this transaction was made public in the canton of Luzern, the people censured the humiliating action of their delegates, and refused to recognize the obligations imposed by the terms of the compromise. Their messengers, despatched into other cantons, stimulated anew the populace to rebellion; but the extravagance of the measures suggested by inexperienced leaders, and their want of concerted action, rendered disaster inevitable when the strength of the confederacy was united against them. Desperate conflicts preceded their final subjugation; but a decisive battle was fought in June, 1653, when General Erlach, with an army of Bernese, encountered the insurgents near Herzogenbuchsee. *Battle of Herzogenbuchsee.* Upon arriving at this point, Erlach discovered that his force was surrounded by antagonists, who were concealed in the neighboring woods; and when he commanded the village to be fired, the desperate peasants fought from burning windows and roofs, and sent death-dealing shots from the falling walls of their homes. When at last they were overpowered, a punishment, universal in extent was decreed, and neither the young for his strength, nor the old for his white hair, was spared. Many were put to death with bitter suffering; upon others heavy fines were imposed, while all who fled were declared outlaws of the empire. The three men who had personated the heroes of Rütli were shot or executed, and Emmenegger was summarily hung.

The Peasants' Revolt had hardly been subdued when religious differences in the confederacy were fanned into a flame, and war again burst forth. A number of families in the canton of Schwyz had secretly embraced Protestantism, and this fact having transpired, their lives were threatened by the authorities, and they fled for safety to Zurich. To secure their possessions in Schwyz, they begged the mediation of Zurich magistrates, and by the government of that canton, property claims against Schwyz were accordingly advanced. Schwyz responded by the confiscation of everything belonging to the fugitives, and, while the magistrates also imprisoned or put to death relatives of the thirty-six families who had fled, they proclaimed that for actions within their own boundaries they would render account only to God and to their own people.

No further impulse was necessary to induce the reformed cantons to take up arms, and **Religious Antagonisms.** Catholic members of the confederacy were equally prompt in preparation for the conflict. The campaign was chiefly characterized by deeds of pillage and plunder,

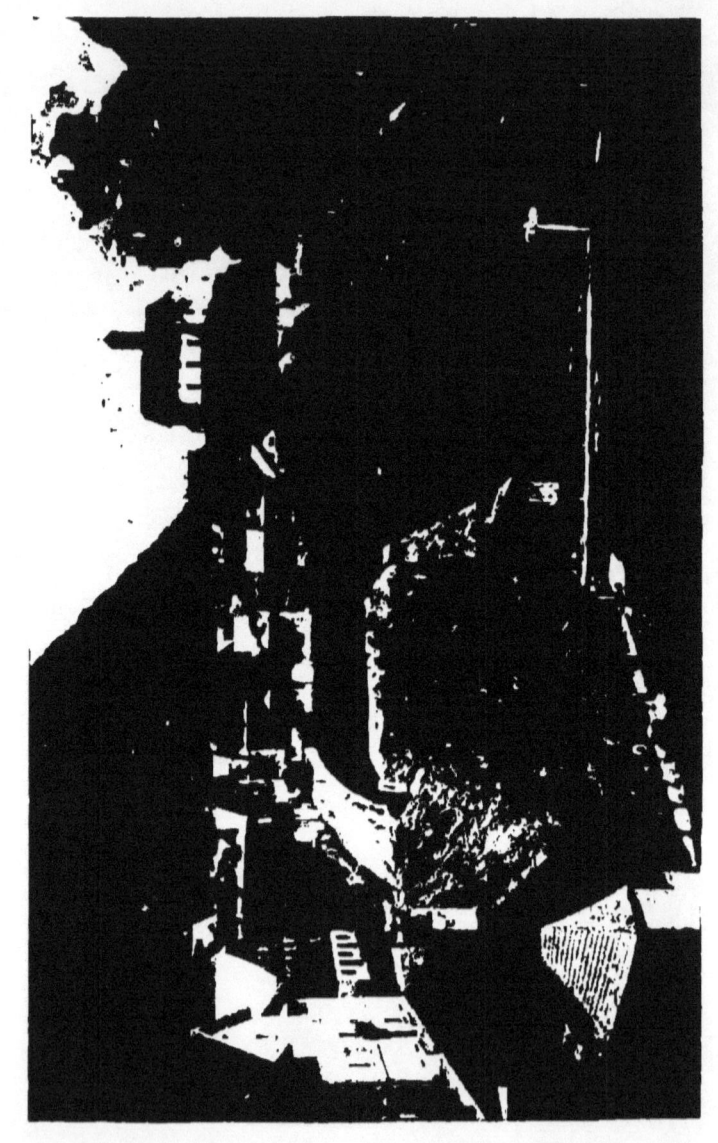

WESEN.

and among the troops from the Reformed cantons so little discipline existed, that a force of twelve thousand Bernese, surprised at Villmergen by four thousand Luzerners, was thrown into confusion, and easily routed. *Battle of Villmergen.* Shortly after the attack, orders to avoid a conflict, as peace negotiations were in progress, were delivered to the commander of the Catholic army, Colonel Pfyffer, but he failed to read the official document when it was delivered, and pursuit of the flying enemy was continued, until eight hundred of their number had been slain. The peace then consummated restored to individual cantons the same authority in religious matters that had been previously possessed, and secured only a temporary tranquillity. A violent antagonism, which resisted diplomacy, had been awakened among the confederates, and slight causes of dispute insured a renewal of hostilities.

When the war of the Spanish Succession divided the nations of Europe by strong partisanship, troops from Luzern were secured for the armies of Louis XIV. In their passage through Thurgau, a band of these soldiers, entered, with drawn swords, a Protestant church in Rapperswyl. A frightened woman, escaping from the building, rushed through the streets and into a neighboring village, shrieking for help. The people in both districts seized their arms, and five Luzerners were killed. When this episode was reported, the Catholic cantons called out their troops, and demanded from the opposite party a heavy recompense. In Zurich, and other Protestant cities, collections were taken in the churches to defray expenses thus entailed; but all propitiatory measures failed where so wide a ground for dispute existed, and a second so-called "religious war" was soon precipitated.

<small>Second "Religious War."</small>

In territory formerly owned by the Counts of Toggenburg, privileges early secured to the peasantry had been greatly curtailed after the purchase of the land by the Abbots of St. Gall. These ecclesiastics, strengthened by alliances with Schwyz and Glaris, ventured to ignore, by degrees, the known franchises of their people, and in the middle of the seventeenth century, the Abbot Leodegar, claimed absolute lordship upon his estates. His oppressive rule at last induced the peasants to carry their grievances before the Swiss Diet; and soon the Toggenburg question became a serious one in the cantons. As the population of the district included both Protestants and Catholics, partisanship of either side

<small>The Toggenburg Question.</small>

was largely determined by religious sympathy, while the recent alliance consummated between Austria and the Abbot excited against the latter a strong personal prejudice.

Perplexity increased as the prerogatives on both sides were discussed, and diet after diet assembled and adjourned without settling the Toggenburg question. Finally the Emperor asserted his superior right to decide the dispute, claiming the district as a fief of the empire, but Zurich and Bern repudiated the imperial claim, asserting that the territory lay within Swiss boundaries, and power to arbitrate for the people rested with the confederates alone. At last the Toggenburgers rose in revolt against the Abbot's officials, and drove them from the land. Leodegar sought to regain his authority by force of arms, but succeeded only in eliciting a declaration of war from the peasantry, who, supported in the action by Bern and Zurich, besieged the castle of the Abbot, and ravaged the district of St. Gall. Then the Catholic cantons prepared to enter the field, and, aided by gold from the papal nuncio, and by the consecrated bullets and amulets freely distributed among their men they assembled a large army, while princes of the empire were hastily summoned to the aid of the exiled Abbot.

To support Bern and Zurich, other Protestant cantons sent troops, and soon, arrayed in hostile ranks, stood a larger number of confederates than had ever been united against a foreign foe. Treachery was not unknown, and in the face of proposed treaties for peace surprises were plotted. After a series of minor encounters, the decisive battle occurred, as in the first campaign, near Villmergen. The two armies, almost equal in numbers, contended for nearly ten hours with fatal bitterness. Victory for the Catholics seemed insured, when, by a manœuvre of the Protestant general — Duval — one division of the adverse army was separated from its main body, and the position of the antagonists was swiftly reversed. Disastrous confusion occurred in Catholic ranks, and two thousand corpses covered the battlefield, when, pressed on every side, they were forced to sue for peace. Both parties had lost valued commanders, and both desired a final cessation of hostilities, when negotiations were opened at Aarau.

By the terms of peace accepted, Protestant control was secured in Baden, Thurgau, Sargans, and the Rheinthal, but only slight alleviation of burdens was

## Freedom from the Empire

obtained for the Toggenburg peasants, whose grievances had been the ostensible cause of the war. The Abbot, indeed, remained in exile, refusing to recognize the terms of the treaty; but after his death, in 1718, the territory was restored to his successor, upon condition of a grant of franchises to the people. The Pope never recognized the treaty, although compelled to recall the nuncio, who had been a leading instigator of the disastrous dissensions.

The moral influence of the war upon the people of Switzerland was deplorable. The cantons, separated by mutual jealousies and hatred, sought sympathy and support in foreign alliances. Bern entered into a treaty with England, while the Catholics were promised aid from France in forcing from their brother confederates a renunciation of lands acquired in the religious wars. "In a political and social light," writes the Swiss historian, Daguet, "the eighteenth century is one of the saddest in our history."

# CHAPTER XX

## PROGRESS IN POLITICAL ENFRANCHISE-MENT

### 1712-1796

ALTHOUGH for nearly a century succeeding the Villmergen wars, the Swiss territory remained nominally undisturbed by domestic or foreign strife, yet religious and political differences continued to separate the people. Jealous cantonal governments, suspicious and critical of one another, justified themselves in the pursuit of individual prosperity, regardless of the effect upon the confederacy at large. The Diet had avoided entanglement in the political game of the Spanish Succession war, but rival parties, in various cantons advocated respectively the French or the Austrian claims, and rendered continually imminent volcanic disturbances.

France had assumed proprietary rights in Switzerland, since the consummation of the treaty that secured her an annual subsidy of Swiss troops, and in return for her payment of

MALOJA.

## Political Enfranchisement 227

gold exacted from the people an undeviating allegiance.[1] If this was not voluntarily rendered, efforts were made to enforce it, and the French ambassador did not hesitate to use violent measures for the accomplishment of his purpose. An instance of his arbitrary proceedings was made public when a son of Thomas Massner, a wealthy citizen of Chur, was kidnapped in Geneva, and placed under strict confinement because his father had expressed sympathy for Austria. Massner retaliated by seizing the person of a French official at Chur, but his act was loudly denounced as a violation of the law of nations. An exchange of prisoners having been arranged, the Frenchman was set at liberty, but the deluded father failed to find his son. He then plotted a more sure revenge, and succeeded in capturing the Duc de Vendôme, grand-prior of France, whom he delivered to the Austrians. For this act France demanded from the government of the Grisons an indemnification, and efforts to negotiate an exchange of prisoners were again put forth. These proved futile, and, to pacify the French,

[1] " Sire," said Louvois to Louis XIV., " With all the gold the French have given to the Swiss, the road from Paris to Basle might be well paved ! " "Sire," responded a Swiss officer who was present, " With all the blood shed by the Swiss for the French, a canal from Basle to Paris might be well filled."

the government of Grisons was obliged to banish Massner, to destroy his house, and to confiscate his property. With a price upon his head, the fugitive sought refuge in Austria, and when, after years had elapsed, he ventured to re-enter Switzerland he was immediately claimed by the French ambassador, and again forced to seek safety in a foreign land. His life ended in exile, and only after the peace of Aix-la-Chapelle had closed the contest between France and Austria was young Massner released from captivity.

In the large cities of Switzerland the seventeenth century marked the growth of a new aristocracy. After the acquisition by Bern of the district of Vaud, the canton abandoned its antique custom of burgher assemblies, and relegated public affairs to the decisions of a Great Council. As time passed on, membership in this body was claimed as an hereditary right among three hundred and sixty families of the city, and when male heirs failed, the office was frequently bestowed, as a marriage portion, upon daughters.

Although the government of Bern was distinguished for its probity and power, an effort to establish a more liberal form of administration was made in 1742, and a demand was

## Political Enfranchisement

forwarded to the council for prerogatives guaranteed to the citizens by the Charter of Berchthold of Zeringen. This petition the magistrates elected to regard as an act of insubordination, and the twenty-six burghers who had signed it were summarily arrested or banished. Samuel Henzi, one of the exiled men, returned to Bern at the expiration of his term of proscription, and headed there a band of malcontents, who were working to establish burgher authority. The aim of the leader was honestly directed at the removal of abuses in the government, but many joined him whose object was less laudable, and Henzi found himself unable to stem the tide of criminal schemes concocted by members of his train. He sought, by flight, to escape responsibility for deeds he disapproved; but revelations that caused his arrest had already been made to the government, and, as leader of the inculpated band, Henzi suffered the contumely that attached itself to the most revolting of their projects. With two companions, Werner and Fuetor, he was beheaded, while others, less prominent in the conspiracies, were banished. The council of Bern, aroused by these events to a realization of danger, proposed a free discussion of

*1749.*

*Disturbances in Bern.*

state affairs, and eventually the burgher class in that city gained a wider influence.

In Freyburg, as in Bern, an oligarchical rule had limited the freedom of early years, and in **Insurrection in Freyburg.** 1784 the "secret families" who composed the council, excluded all others from entrance into their coterie. The people vainly recalled the days of old, when in one district alone the city boasted of two thousand tanners, and when more than two thousand pieces of cloth were annually woven for exportation to Venice. In vain the burghers sought release from the decrees of autocratic magistrates, and at last an embassy of sixty men, under Nicholas Chenaux, was deputed to present complaints before the council. When this measure proved ineffectual to procure a redress of grievances, adherents from the adjacent country were notified, and three thousand insurgents, bearing consecrated banners, encamped before the city walls.

The council begged aid of Bern, and troops from that city, promptly despatched, led the Freyburg council to a swift victory. Chenaux, fleeing with his troops, was struck down by a member of his own band and delivered to his pursuers, who mounted his head upon the gateway of Freyburg. Having visited with severe punishment all known to be implicated in the revolt, the government then invited a presentation of complaints from the people; but no satisfactory concessions were allowed when delegates from various districts were despatched to Freyburg, and the position taken by Bern, Luzern, and Solothurn dissipated all hope of the favorable mediation of other cantons. These three influential states declared themselves prepared to maintain the Constitution of Freyburg, and, although recommending that the burdens of the country people should be lightened, stigmatized the demands of the burgher class as both "groundless and unconstitutional." This sentence was promulgated from the pulpits, and terminated all public exhibition of dissatisfaction; but Chenaux was regarded as a martyr, and pilgrimages, which the government was powerless to prevent, were regularly made to his grave.

In the small territory of Geneva, where Voltaire remarked that by shaking his wig he powdered the republic, permanence of government had been secured by a clause in the constitution which decreed the death penalty to any one who should suggest a modification of the laws. But as increased wealth and distinction were acquired by the citizens, a new aristocracy arose who revived ancient patrician customs, and claimed exclusive privileges.[1]

The councils of Twenty-five and of Two Hundred were largely swayed by this class, and in 1717, without consulting the citizens in general assembly, the magistrates, to defray the expenses attending repairs upon the city fortifications, imposed a new tax. This was strenuously opposed by the burghers, and their cause was powerfully espoused by Micheli of Crest, a member of the Great Council. For his published criticism of magisterial ordinances, Micheli was deprived of his position in the assembly, and threatened with imprisonment, and although he sought safety in flight, he was hung in effigy, and his writings were torn by the hangman. But opposition was not overborne by these ultra measures; the citizens continued to demand the repeal of the tax, and in 1734 the council called upon Bern for aid in enforcing their unpopular decrees. Then a mob took possession of the highway by which the Bernese must advance, and convoked there a general council; but influence was exerted which secured the vote

*Excitements in Geneva.*

---

[1] In 1697 a decree was passed in the council "d'empêcher que l'on donne aussi facilement le titre de madame aux femmes de toutes conditions."

## Political Enfranchisement 233

of a majority for the completion of the fortifications of their city, and the consequent imposition of the tax for ten years, and upon this basis a compromise was effected and temporary peace secured. But the volcanic condition of the city was again revealed when the populace demanded the banishment of the syndic Trembly, against whom, as director of the fortifications, hostile sentiments had long been accumulating. Again the burghers took up arms, and only through the mediation of Bern, Zurich, and France, was tranquillity restored. The French ambassador, with the assistance of delegates from the two cantons, then undertook to prepare a new constitution for the distracted city. By its decree the power of the aristocracy and the authority of the smaller councils were restricted, and a peace, which endured for a quarter of a century, was bequeathed to Geneva.

1738.

In 1762, a native of Geneva, though long a wanderer, the "man in convulsions," Jean Jacques Rousseau, had so excited the Parisian world that his books were burned by the hangman. Geneva imitated the example of the French, and refused to consider the remonstrances presented by a number of her citizens. The disputes, thus inaugurated, served as sparks to kindle fires whose fuel had long been accumulating, and the two antagonistic parties known as Representatives and Negatives held riotous meetings, and multiplied their grounds of dispute until the magistrates again threatened to seek foreign intervention. This method of arbitration was odious to both disputants, and to prevent its adoption they agreed in registering an act of pacification which entitled the burghers to greater authority than they had formerly possessed in minor matters of legislation, and gave them power to elect one-half the members of the Great Council. But the aristocratic party, unwilling to relinquish their perquisites, endeavored, during eight years, to evade the fulfilment of their contract, and, intriguing with the French, sought from that government support in their usurpations. Plots and counterplots overlapped one another, party strife waxed hot and violent, and at last the intervention of the former arbiters was requested. Zurich refused her aid in the crisis, but Bern, Sardinia, and France stationed troops in Geneva. From "Les Délices," the country-seat of Voltaire, the French battalions pointed their guns against the fair city, while the arbiters, sentencing seven members of the aristocracy to perpetual banishment, established the authority of the "Negatives," who immediately proscribed "secret societies, military exercises, and recent books."

At this period, in close proximity to the tumultuous city, the cyclone of revolution was sweeping away all landmarks of ancient usage, and solving political problems with unauthorized legislation. A similarity of language rendered the dissemination of French ideas easy in Geneva, and soon peasants of the surrounding country united in a demand for the annexation of their territory to France. Incited by the spirit of their neighbors, a bolder band organized independent tribunals, and by such authority banished or put to death all obnoxious persons. Anarchy once more prevailed, but, in 1794, too weary of the long confusion for further conflict, the citizens adopted a new constitution, *Changing Constitutions in Geneva.* which invested syndics and councils with an authority long denied them. The inauguration of this form of government was officially announced to Bern and to Zurich, but the magistrates in those cantons hesitated to give it recognition, and their doubts of its permanence were justified. Again, with the rise of breadstuffs and other commodities, tumults occurred; the arsenals were seized, and the magistrates imprisoned. Again, by the failure of both parties to attain their objective positions, concessions were forced from antagonistic factions. In 1796 another constitution was framed, which gave to all persons born on Genevese territory equal prerogatives, and upon this basis tranquillity was maintained for two years. At the end of that period the fortunes of war united Geneva to France.

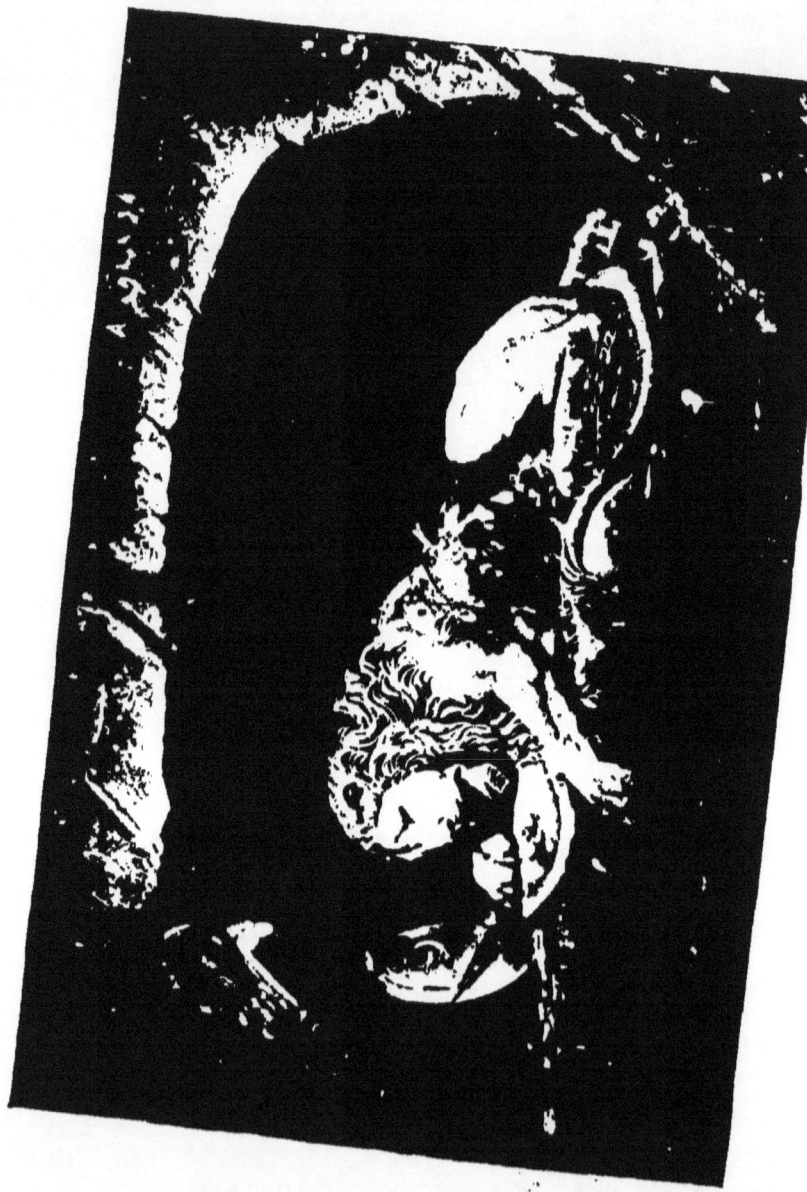
LION OF LUZERN.

## CHAPTER XXI

### THE ERA OF THE FRENCH REVOLUTION

#### 1789-1820

"WE are Swiss! and the Swiss never surrender but with their lives!" were words that the world heard, even through the clang and clamor of demoniacal Paris in 1792, for they were a defiance to peril and to death, uttered by the leader of eight hundred heroic men, whose martyrdom Luzern's carved rock records.

The report of the massacre of the Tuileries guard sent through Switzerland a prolonged quiver of that political earthquake, that, advancing in swift waves, had already shaken the confederacy. The aggressive tendency of French revolutionary tribunals was keenly realized in the cantons, and the governments hesitated to offend a nation who were disposed to offer only a Pandora-box to the world at large; consequently, the Diet was prompt in the recognition of forms of legislation, successively established on territory adjacent to its own.

But in the midst of the maelstrom of reaction from established constitutional rule, many cantonal governments endeavored to preserve their authority by an increased severity of administration, and through this impolitic course precipitated the crisis they were seeking to avert.

When the inhabitants of Staeffa, on the shore of Lake Zurich, manifested an inclination to obtain civil enfranchisement, the village was immediately occupied by a military force, and the people oppressed by heavy fines. The magistrates of Grisons exercised so imperious and rigorous an authority over the Valtelina that the occupants of that valley sought the interference of Napoleon in their behalf. His demand that the district should be admitted as a fourth member of the Grison league having been disregarded, the autocrat summarily annexed it to the newly-organized Cisalpine Republic.

Among the Vaudois, a people little disposed to political excitement, the temper of opposition to foreign domination had been induced and stimulated by a few wealthy men, at whose head stood the refugee, Francis Cæsar La Harpe. Antagonism to the sway of Bern was rapidly developed, and when Napoleon traversed the Pays de Vaud, on his way to the congress of Rastadt, triumphal arches greeted him, bearing inscriptions quoted from his verdict in the Valtelina: "One nation cannot be subject to another, without violation of the principles of national and of public rights."

At the instigation of the "Helvetic Club" of Paris, French troops were sent, in 1798, to the shores of Lake Geneva, and a transitory result was the establishment by the Vaudois of a "Lemanic Republic." Bern, thus despoiled of a province, was divided into two political parties: one led by Frederick Steiger, "the last great man of ancient Switzerland," who advocated resistance to foreign encroachments, while a powerful faction under French influence insisted upon the superior policy of peace-negotiations. Meanwhile, an army was advancing from Vaud, under General Brune, and troops sent to oppose its progress fought ineffectually, or fled before facing the foe. The Diet, which had assembled in alarm, separated in the distraction of fear; mutual distrust of one another had been too long fostered in the cantons, and no united effort could now be anticipated. Gradually France appropriated districts within Swiss boundaries, and unceremoniously assumed the right to dismem-

*The Lemanic Republic.*

ber the confederacy. On the advance of French troops, Luzern, Schaffhausen, and Zurich declared their dependencies free, and released their prisoners. Bern received into her aristocratic council fifty-two representatives from the country, and Freyburg agreed to make equal concessions. But the foreign foe pursued his unimpeded way, and, as he moved, his inflexible grasp covered each canton in turn, closing upon each the iron door that stifled every whisper of opposition. Solothurn and Freyburg fell, and Bern was summoned to surrender. The city magistrates replied by arming twenty-five hundred troops to confront fifteen hundred of the enemy; but by the crafty Brune the superior forces were beguiled with peace propositions until the army of the Rhine, under Schauenburg, had joined its strength to his. Then Bern, surrounded by foes, was forced to capitulate, and to yield to the invaders all her garnered wealth. While French soldiers, proclaiming themselves liberators of the people, *Dissolution of the Confederacy.* pillaged the land, the French Directory declared: "The confederacy is no more!" and arbitrarily dissolving the union of five hundred years, inaugurated *1798.* upon the territory a new "Helvetic Republic." This state, "one and indivisible,"

# Era of the French Revolution

was partitioned into nineteen cantons,[1] and four deputies from each received power to exercise legislative authority in a Grand Council and a Senate, while the central executive authority was vested in a Directory of five members, holding its seat at Luzern. *The Helvetic Republic.*

Neither the civil nor religious liberties for which the Swiss had contended were infringed by the new constitution, but against the acceptance of any ordinances imposed by a conqueror the spirit of the nation rebelled. The three Waldstätten, with Zug, Appenzell, and Glarus, recalling their ancient traditions and the deeds of heroic ancestors, leagued together once again to resist subjugation. "In battle and in blood," they said, "our fathers won the glorious jewel of our independence, and we will not lose it but in battle and in blood." Led by the valiant Aloys Reding, a hero descended from heroes, they joined in solemn oaths of fidelity unto death, and marched to meet the intruding army. Overpowered in two encounters, they rallied for the third at Rosenthurm, near the field of Morgarten, where an enemy four times their numbers confronted them. *Battle of Rosenthurm.*

---

[1] A name then officially used in Switzerland for the first time.

Thrice on that memorable ground the foe was repulsed, but, although "every Swiss soldier fought like a Cæsar," the little band of patriots was finally overpowered, the oath of allegiance to the new constitution was forced upon each district, and "the first year of Swiss slavery" opened.

<small>1798.</small>

The nation was not blind to the fact that its fall had been due to the indulgence of selfish greed for individual cantonal aggrandizement and the consequent weakening of the tie that had formerly upheld the confederation; but in spite of this conviction, local antagonisms continued to be fostered, and no efforts were made to allay the spirit of discontent fomented among the masses by the new division of land. When oaths of allegiance to the new government were required, numerous outbreaks occurred, for the French commissioners, living in luxury and extravagance at the expense of the country, regarded neither the unpaid salaries of the clergy, nor the poverty of the people, and the Executive Directory, established at Aarau, commanded neither confidence nor respect.

The ecclesiastics of Nidwalden, anticipating the abolition of the monasteries, declared that the new constitution was the work of Satan, and quickly excited a formidable disturbance.

Led by a Capuchin monk, named Paul Steiger, the peasants at Stanz offered desperate resistance to the French troops; but after a conflict of ten hours they were overcome, and, by the merciless punishment that followed, nearly four thousand victims perished amid their burning homes.

In the autumn of 1798, after a victory over the French in Swabia, an Austrian army entered Switzerland. In alarm at the proximity of this foe, the Helvetic government quitted Luzern, and sought security at Bern; but French troops soon encountered the Austrian force, and Switzerland again became a theatre of foreign war, while in both antagonistic armies Swiss soldiers were enrolled, to oppose their brothers in a bitter strife. Swiftly the French were expelled from Schwyz, and the Austrians, with their Russian allies, advanced toward Zurich. The Abbot of St. Gall, confidently anticipating the resumption of his former authority, deprived his people, prematurely, of their charter, and forced them again into slavery. But Massena met the Russians, and the tide of victory turned; the French entered Zurich, again masters of the country, while Austrians and Russians were in full retreat; and during three succeeding years a French army, quartered upon the people, reduced them to a condition of poverty unknown before in their history. Powerless in this humiliation to resist the bayonets of their oppressors, they made their misery manifest by four attempts to effect changes in their government; and insurrectionists insisted upon a restoration of ancient forms, even after the treaty of Amiens (1802) had withdrawn foreign garrisons from the country. The unprotected government officials fled to Lausanne, and a Diet was summoned to meet in Schwyz for the establishment of the old constitution.

But the sovereign power of France was yet dominant, and Napoleon commanded peace. His ambassadors arrived at Lausanne, and immediately the malcontents laid down their arms, burgher and magistrate bowing silently before the messenger of the First Consul. In an address to the Swiss, through General Rapp, Napoleon dwelt upon the anarchy that had so long prevailed among them, and declared that only the country's desperate need induced him to retract his resolution against interfering in its affairs. He offered to mediate, upon condition that within five days three deputies, accompanied by delegates from the cantons, should be sent to Paris.

"Every rational man," he said, "must perceive that my mediation is a blessing conferred upon Switzerland by that Providence which, amid so many concurring causes of social dissolution, has always preserved your national existence and independence. It would be painful to think that destiny has singled out this epoch, which has called to life so many new republics, as the hour of destruction to one of the oldest communities in Europe."

The Helvetic senate replied in a spirit of gratitude and submission; cantonal deputies were immediately chosen, and in December, 1803, the sixty-three Swiss delegates in Paris were informed by letter of the basis upon which Napoleon would consent to mediate in their behalf.

The "Act of Mediation," provided for the addition to the thirteen old members of the confederation of six new cantons; two of these, St. Gall and Grisons, having formerly been "associates," and the remaining four, Aargau, Ticino, Thurgau, and Vaud, to be formed from subject territory, which had been at various periods conquered. In this confederacy of nineteen members, a central government, resembling the old Diet, but with functions enlarged, should direct national affairs at the cities of Freyburg, Bern, *The "Act of Mediation."*

Solothurn, Basle, Zurich, and Luzern, in annual rotation; each canton, during the period of its pre-eminence, assuming the name of *Vorort*, or directorial canton, while the burgomaster of the distinguished city became president of the confederation with the title of "Landammann of Switzerland." Independent cantonal sovereignty was to be restored, directed in Democratic districts by *Landesgemeinden*, and in other cantons by "great" and "small" councils, but no exclusive privileges, either for families or cities, would be tolerated. Freedom in trade, and license to establish himself according to his pleasure, should be the prerogative of every inhabitant of the land, and full liberty of worship was granted to Protestants and Catholics alike.

In this document, which also stated the provisions of a close alliance with France, the name "Switzerland," was for the first time officially employed. The prescribed conditions were accepted by the deputies at Paris, and, the dissolution of the Helvetic government having been formally proclaimed, French troops were withdrawn from Swiss territory. Allegiance to the new order of things was promptly tendered, except in the canton of Zurich, where, on the ground of diffi-

*Name of "Switzerland."*

## Era of the French Revolution 247

culties concerning the redemption of titles, ground-rents, etc., the officials authorized to demand the oath of acceptance, met resistance. But the opposition was speedily quelled, and six years of tranquillity followed. A stronger sense of fellowship had been promoted by the common trials through which the cantons had passed, and enterprises of mutual advantage were projected. In 1807 the great work was proposed of draining twenty-eight thousand acres of annually-inundated swamp-land, and within a few years an unhealthy valley was converted into an attractive and habitable district, while the water there accumulated formed the navigable channel of the great Linth Canal. Meanwhile, schools were *The Linth Canal.* multiplied; industrial and commercial pursuits, untrammelled, prospered; each canton sent cheerfully its contingent to guard the frontier, while the Diet declared its unanimous resolution, by the maintenance of a strict neutrality in European disputes, to preserve the tranquillity of the land.

In 1806 Napoleon gave Neuchâtel to his general, Berthier, and in 1810 the Swiss were again made to feel the authority of the capricious autocrat, for, on the plea that the possession of the Simplon was essential to France and to Italy, a decree was issued, incorporating the Valais with the French empire, and, although the Diet protested against this robbery, they were powerless to resist it. Their contract to furnish France with an uninterrupted contingent of sixteen thousand troops had, through the constant warfare of Napoleon, become an agreement burdensome beyond toleration. In 1807, the promised number being incomplete, a conscription was ordered by the Emperor, and to avoid this measure the cantons took the desperate course of emptying the prisons to fill up the regiments.

When the star of the great commander sank in "the battle of the nations," at Leipsic, the hour seemed to have struck for the re-establishment of Swiss independence; but, ignoring the pledged neutrality of the country, the allied sovereigns, *en route* for Paris, attempted to traverse Switzerland with their victorious armies. Suddenly, from the Diet, an edict was promulgated which withdrew home troops from the Rhine frontier, and allowed the allies unimpeded passage. In many cities the wealthy classes welcomed the presence of the foreigners, anticipating from them support in efforts to re-establish the old system of aristocratic sovereignty and peasant

<small>1813.</small>

servitude. Bern, Solothurn, Freyburg, and Luzern declared the "Act of Mediation" annulled, and claimed their former dominion over adjacent districts. Zurich headed an opposition to this assumption of authority, and in various localities tumults, which the local authorities were impotent to suppress, became of such frequent occurrence that the "Long Diet" continued at Zurich, seemed the only tie to prevent the dismemberment of the nation.

Meanwhile the allied sovereigns had entered Paris; Napoleon was at Elba, and the congress assembled at Vienna began its peace deliberations. Ambassadors from Switzerland were despatched to this assembly, where an intention to guarantee the perpetual neutrality of Swiss territory was announced; but, before the pledge could be fulfilled, the tramp of armies and the roar of artillery once more aroused the world, for Napoleon had returned, and again monarchs trembled. *Congress of Vienna.*

This interlude was a brief one; the day of Waterloo came and passed (June 18, 1815), and the reassembled Congress of Vienna, recognizing the new act of confederation adopted by a majority of the Swiss cantons, agreed to recompense the confederacy for districts detached from their territory by the new divisions of Europe, excepting only Chiavenna, Valtelina, and Bormio, which, though claimed by the Grisons, had been annexed to Austria.

The entrance of the allies had delivered Geneva, Valais, and Neuchâtel from French domination, and, by vote of the "Long Diet" of 1814, they were joined with the Swiss Confederation. In 1707, Neuchâtel, to escape the grasp of Louis XIV., had voluntarily placed itself under the ducal sway of Prussia, and now appeared both as a Swiss canton, and a Hohenzollern principality. Napoleon had restored Ticino to the Swiss, and twenty-two cantons formed the nation whose deputies to the Congress solemnly presented a Federal Pact, formulated in the Diet at Zurich. Its terms were accepted by the allies, and, by the stipulations of the Peace of Paris, the future inviolability of Swiss territory was guaranteed.

*The Federal Pact of 1815.*

The Federal Pact of 1815 formed the sixth constitution given to the Swiss nation since the formation of the confederacy in 1291. As a fundamental principle, the pact declared that no community could hold any subject-district; no form of vassalage should be allowed. The Diet was to meet, hence-

*Nov. 20, 1815.*

forth, by turn, at Bern, Zurich, and Luzern. One vote in this assembly was apportioned to each canton, and the sovereign right of each state in its own territory was distinctly recognized.

Freed from the distractions of continental warfare, the people willingly relegated to their deputies the settlement of all minor questions, either of Church or of State, and from 1815 to 1820 no political movement of importance disturbed the tranquillity of the land. Social and intellectual pursuits prospered, cantons vied with one another in enthusiasm for educational advantages; steamboats appeared upon the lakes of Geneva, Neuchâtel, and Constance; within Swiss boundaries new philanthropic schemes were liberally sustained, while cordial aid was extended to the Greeks, whose struggle to free themselves from the Turkish sovereignty excited a sympathetic interest throughout Switzerland.

## CHAPTER XXII

### THE LEAGUE OF ROTHEN

#### 1830–1847

THE political life of Switzerland, like that of other European nations, was struck into rapid vibration by the shock of the French revolution of 1830, and once again the masses rose to combat the power of the aristocracy. Again the prizes to be obtained were revised constitutions, with broader definitions of popular rights, and within a few months twelve cantons modified their laws, some peaceably, others after fierce contentions.

Throughout this revolutionary period in cantonal governments, the federal constitution of the Swiss remained unaltered; but in 1832, in response to increasing evidence of popular desire, the Diet empowered a committee of fifteen to formulate a new covenant. In honor of the delegate from Geneva, who held the position of secretary to this commission, the document prepared was entitled the Rossi Pact. It was strongly supported in many districts, but failed of acceptance through the opposition of a few cantons, led by Luzern.

*The Rossi Pact.*

During the period of universal agitation attending the discussion of this subject, the canton of Basle had been immersed in civil strife. The refusal of magistrates to grant to the country people a representation proportional to their numbers, led to hostilities which culminated in bloodshed. The city of Basle then united with the smaller cantons of Switzerland in a league known as the Sarnenbund, which was organized for the purpose of presenting a united opposition to all radical tendencies. The rejection of the Rossi Pact encouraged the members of this league to open hostilities against liberal governments, and its first measure was the expulsion from cantonal union, by a legislative vote, of forty-two antagonistic communes, while sixteen hundred troops were put into the field to suppress opposition. The *Vorort* of the confederacy protested against these measures, but her troops, sent as mediators, were refused admission into the city of Basle. Then the seven large cantons formed the league of the

*The Sarnenbund.*

Siebnerbund, and offered opposition, while the Diet ordered sixteen thousand troops to occupy the canton of Basle. Despite the attempted intervention of foreign ambassadors, the dissolution of the Sarnenbund was decreed, and Basle was divided into the two half cantons of Basel-Stadt, and Basel-Landschaft. Each division was privileged to send one deputy to the Diet, but each was entitled to only half a vote; hence, in case of opposition between the districts, the influence of the canton was annulled. In Neuchâtel, at this period, two parties, equally opposed to their double *régime*, endeavored on the one hand to achieve a severance from Prussia, and on the other a separation from Switzerland. The former counted upon the sympathy of the Swiss Diet; but that authority, recognizing the claims of their early compact, sent troops to support the existing government, and the attempted revolution failed.

<small>The Siebnerbund.</small>

In 1817, Switzerland had entered the "Holy Alliance," organized by Alexander of Russia for the maintenance of political and religious toleration; but the friendly reception now offered by the cantons to foreign refugees gave offence to arbitrary potentates, and called forth many remonstrances. In 1833 five hundred

Poles, who had secretly procured arms at Geneva, attempted an invasion of Savoy from Swiss territory, and, although the episode was barren of result, Sardinia, Austria, and some members of the Rhine Confederation were induced to enter formal complaints against the Confederate government, and to demand the expulsion from their domain of all disturbers of European peace. Disputes over these exactions, and minor matters, resulted in a temporary interruption of friendly intercourse with Germany; but in 1835, upon the accession of Ferdinand I. to the throne of Austria, a reconciliation was effected. *Difficulties with Foreign Governments.*

A more serious exigency for the Confederacy arose from a demand enforced in the name of M. Thiers, then premier of France, for the expulsion from Switzerland of a refugee named Conseil, who was stigmatized as a dangerous agitator.

When this requirement had been conceded, it was discovered that the supposititious refugee was in reality a spy sent into Switzerland by the French government. The indignation naturally expressed throughout the cantons was met by angry menaces from the Duke of Montebello, the French ambassador, and serious consequences were averted only through skilful diplomacy.

The hazards of this affair were followed by other complications consequent upon the prolonged residence of Louis Napoleon upon Swiss territory. Hortense Beauharnais had sought there an asylum, and her son became a naturalized citizen of Thurgau, serving as captain in the federal army. In 1837 an unsuccessful attempt to gain the allegiance of the French nation drew down upon the young man a sentence of exile that carried him to America. Upon his reappearance in Thurgau, France demanded his expulsion, but the Thurgau deputy claimed that as a citizen of that canton the prince-presumptive could insist upon protection so long as he remained inoffensive. The Diet, divided in opinion, submitted the question to the cantons, but France, impatient of this leisurely proceeding, despatched twenty-five hundred men against the Swiss, who were characterized in her angry proclamation as "turbulent neighbors."

This language roused the Swiss to a fierce antagonism. Geneva and Vaud flew to arms; the French border was guarded by defiant and enthusiastic forces, while one by one the cantons voted to resist the demands of France, and to maintain the right of their nation to independent judgment upon the point in dispute. But the Prince Napoleon, unwilling to compromise the country so long his asylum, sent a letter to the Diet, announcing his voluntary departure from the land, and France, with protestations of friendship toward Switzerland, called home her troops.

The decree of 1835, which ordained public sessions of the Diet, was a measure abetting the advance of popular freedom, and it had also tended to induce co-operation among the cantons, for the promotion of education, military discipline, and other matters *1838.* of common advantage; but with the cessation of foreign disagreements, internal jealousies revived, and these were soon augmented by religious disputes.

At the close of the Reformation, seven cantons remained in communion with the Roman Church, namely, Luzern, Schwyz, Uri, Unterwalden, Zug, Freyburg, and Solothurn; five were avowedly Protestant — Bern, Basle, Zurich, St. Gall, and Schaffhausen; while the remaining cantons recognized both forms of worship. *Religious Divisions.* In the Helvetic Republic (1798–1803) the exercise of either faith had been permitted, and the Act of Mediation (1803) stipulated for liberty of choice in religious creeds; but the pact of 1815 took no cognizance of ecclesiastical affairs, except in the article guaranteeing convents and chapters.

Rome had never ceased her efforts to regain a universal domination in Switzerland, and in 1814, when a papal nuncio resumed his seat in Luzern, the spirit of freedom alone saved the people from the superstitious subjugation to which their ancestors had yielded. In the midst of the political turmoil of 1838–40 the Catholic party sought to establish a national archbishopric in Switzerland, and thus to secure to their faith a dominating influence; but the project was condemned by the Pope, although not until the excitement it induced had necessitated an exact definition of the limit of clerical interference in State affairs. On this point disputes waxed violent. A decree of the great council, ordaining national supervision of cantonal monasteries, called forth open remonstrances from the abbey of Muri. The magistrates of Schwyz ignored a law forbidding the admission of Jesuits, but stimulated thereby many local animosities; while in Glarus, the decision of the *Landesgemeinde*, denying Catholic clergy an equality of privileges with those of Protestant persuasion, was rejected by a minority in the council, who, in opposition to advisers in Uri, Schwyz, and Unterwalden, refused the oath to their new constitution.

In 1839, Zurich became *Vorort* of the Confederacy, and the Diet was in session when Frederick Strauss accepted the invitation to the chair of theology in the university of that city, pre-eminent for culture. Strauss, who had been educated for the Church, had advanced from the position of a country pastor to the chair of a professor at Maulbrom, and the distinction of lecturer at Tübingen. In 1835 he attained notoriety by the publication of a "Life of Jesus," in which he attempted to show that the Gospel narratives were only a collection of myths, gathered by early communities. The book cost Strauss his professorship at Tübingen, and he retired to private literary life, until called by the Zurich Board of Education to the theological chair in their university. In the storm of opposition that prevented his occupation of this position, the government withdrew its indorsement of the invitation, but failed by the concession to quell the excitement. A "committee of faith" demanded ecclesiastical control in educational affairs, and when the magistrates charged this band with seditious acts, ten thousand men assembled at Kloten and voted for open resistance to the government. A rumor that troops from other cantons had been summoned to aid the authorities of Zurich precipitated a conflict, and messengers hurried through the country calling upon the people to rise in defence of their religion. Led by the pastor, Bernard Huzel, a motley mob of fanatics, in disorderly array, and armed with clubs, scythes, or any weapons they could secure, marched to the gates of Zurich, chanting psalms on their way. Against slight opposition they forced an entrance into the city, but in the cathedral square a force of armed men was encountered, with whom shots were exchanged. At this juncture intelligence arrived that the radical magistrates had abdicated, and the defenders of the city at once withdrew opposition. Burgomaster Hess and other officials united with the insurgents, a conservative government took the seats of the recent rulers, the committee of faith called upon the people to recognize the victory vouchsafed to the just cause, and for several days Zurich was given up to a celebration in which religious services mingled with excited carousals.

*Religious Conflicts in Zurich.*

The re-election of local officials served to propagate the temper of intolerance, which

GOESCHENEN.

## The League of Rothen

spread into other cantons, and impelled similar outbreaks, though less signal results attended them. In the canton of Aargau a grand council of two hundred members had, until 1840, represented, equally the Catholic and Protestant interests. The election of delegates without reference to creed caused, in 1841, a numerical advantage on the Protestant side, and Augustine Keller, deputy from Aargau proposed, before the Diet, the abolition of religious houses, which he characterized as "hearthstones of strife." In defence of these objects of their veneration, two thousand peasants took up arms at Villmergen, but, at the hands of government troops, suffered an overwhelming defeat. The elections of 1842 showed a majority in sympathy with the views of Keller, and the suppression of convents in Aargau followed; but in 1843 Luzern became *Vorort*, and the preponderating influence in the confederacy swung to the Catholic side.

*Religious Conflicts in Aargau.*

The guaranteed pact of 1815 was quoted, and the State council of Luzern issued a mandate annulling all sales of convent property. In the midst of a wide-spread tumult a special meeting of the Diet was summoned, but, sustained by the Bernese government, Aargau refused to revoke her decree, claiming that the welfare of the canton was impaired, and even its existence imperilled, by the condemned institutions. After long debate, a compromise was agreed upon, and the re-establishment of a few convents in Aargau produced temporary quiet; although the ejected abbots continued to present annually before the Diet their unrecognized claims.

A radical government had early been established in Luzern, but civil strife was propagated through the influence of a fanatical peasant, named Joseph Leu, who proposed a withdrawal from the league of the confederacy, and the inauguration of a new state, in which the supreme guidance of educational matters should be committed to the Jesuits. Before the excited populace the city magistrates were almost powerless; a draft of the proposed constitution was submitted to the Pope, and, receiving from that potentate a politic expression of his faith in their good intentions, the revolutionists worked on; liberty-trees were planted in cities and villages, State councils fled, and the triumph of the Catholic cause was manifested by the unresisted promulgation of new laws by new magistrates. In 1845 Joseph Leu was assassinated, and, although

*Joseph Leu's Insurrection in Luzern.*

the murderer expiated his crime upon the scaffold, the entire party of Leu's opponents were held responsible for the deed; and, while the peasant was exalted as a saint and martyr, and pilgrimages were made to his grave, persecution and imprisonment was the vengeance visited by the magistrates upon many innocent heads.

One step followed another, each wider in result, and increasingly antagonistic to the *Bund* of the confederacy, until, at Rothen, in September, 1843, Luzern united with the other Catholic cantons in a secret defensive and offensive alliance. Consummated ostensibly for the maintenance of the pact of 1815, this League of Rothen ripened into the *Sonderbund* of 1846, a conspiracy for the establishment of Catholic supremacy throughout Switzerland.

Meanwhile, in the district of Valais, the people had been quietly subservient to their priesthood, or, if aroused to emulate the liberal progress of their neighbors, had encountered a prompt opposition that quenched the spirit of freedom. But gradually demands became more importunate, and local disputes worked toward a crisis in civil affairs. Since 1814 the six German districts of High *（Disturbances in Valais.）*

Valais had been entitled to send twenty-four deputies to the Valaisian diet, while the seven communes of Low Valais, with a population almost double that of High Valais, were allowed only twenty-eight representatives. Low Valais claimed a right to representation proportional to population; High Valais asserted an ancient right to superiority of representation, and voted for separation rather than the relinquishment of these prerogatives. An attempted intervention by the Swiss Diet proved fruitless. Low Valais gained by force of arms an equality of privileges, and in 1840 established her constitution upon that basis. But, encouraged by the clergy, who feared a loss of influence through the progress of liberal pinciples, members of the old council awaited an opportunity to regain authority. The party of "Old Switzerland" opposed the newly-formed society of "Young Switzerland," — an organization hostile to priestly power, and whose members were declared by the clergy to be ineligible to Church privileges. The enmity between the two parties grew more pronounced, and in the elections of 1843 bribes were so freely distributed that the bounds of toleration were overpassed. On their way to the polls a band of "Young Swiss" attacked the printing-office of a paper circulated in the interests of the clergy, while the council called out troops, and summoned confederate aid. At the bridge of Trient a force of "Old Swiss," in ambush, attacked a detachment of liberals, and after a desperate conflict, in which thirty "Young Swiss" were slain, the remainder of their band were forced to fly. The occupation of Lower Valais by the victors followed, and a constitution was established which secured the priests in all their monopolies, gave the superintendence of educational affairs to the Jesuits, and refused liberty of worship. Valais, it declared, must first be Catholic, then Swiss.

Intelligence of these events excited fierce indignation against the Jesuits, and in Aargau a great council voted for the expulsion of the order from Switzerland. The proposition was not intentionally hostile to the Catholic religion, but was regarded as a necessary precaution against undue influence of the priests in civil affairs. When, however, the Aargau deputy presented the measure before the Diet, he found support from the Basle representative alone, while the deputy from Valais was permitted to resume his seat in the council, and his vindication of the action of his canton received but slight criticism. The influence of the "Society of Jesus" was wide in the land,

and when the press too openly revealed the subterfuges practised by that order, its freedom of criticism was checked by legal procedures. But in Vaud, when magistrates, subject to this priestly domination, refused a demand presented by the people for the expulsion of Jesuits from their canton, citizens and militia united against the ruling authorities, and without damage to person or property established a provisional government with a liberal constitution, although the hostile disposition of forty clergymen was manifested by their refusal to read the proclamation of the new magistrates.

<small>Free Corps Expedition.</small>

Meanwhile, in Luzern, the grand council voted in favor of intrusting public education to Jesuit supervision, prohibiting the circulation of newspapers from liberal cantons, and persecuting all who were suspected of holding opinions opposed to the Catholic policy. Encouraged by the fall of the Vaudois government, some Luzerners — exiled since the era of Leu's influence — organized, with their partisans from neighboring cantons, an expedition against the city. A motley troop, known as the Free Corps, under command of Dr. Steiger, a former physician of Luzern, and Ulrich Ochsenbein of Nidau, occupied, without difficulty, the height of the Gütsch, from which point it was proposed to open a cannonade upon the city. But indecision among the leaders caused a delay that proved disastrous to their projects. General Sonnenberg advanced against them with trained troops. In a disorderly conflict the Free Corps suffered defeat, and the number of prisoners carried to Luzern filled the prisons and overflowed into the churches. The city magistrates refused to accept ransom for their captives, rejected the intervention of the *Vorort* of the confederacy, and declared their resolution to eradicate within their domain every tendency to opposition.

Suddenly the veil of secrecy that, since 1843, had enshrouded the league of Rothen was swept aside; and the alliance of the Sonderbund was revealed. In 1846 the seven cantons who had during three years been secretly joined in the league of Rothen declared that in this union they should oppose the strength of the other confederates, until the re-establishment of the Aargau convents was decreed by the Diet, the question of the expulsion of the Jesuits dropped, and all modifications of the federal pact renounced.

"We maintain," said these cantons, "that our league is *not* at variance with the provisions of our confederate pact; it is purely defensive, and has been rendered necessary by aggressions on the part of other cantons. We intend no evil to others if they do not attack us, and we shall maintain our league as long as our own security seems to require."

Hitherto the relation of the confederated cantons had been that of states bound by common loyalty to the articles of their constitution. Now, seven Catholic cantons — Luzern, Schwyz, Uri, Unterwalden, Zug, Freyburg, and Appenzell-Rhodes-Intérieure — maintained the doctrine that each canton was at liberty to interpret for itself the terms of the federal pact. To meet the emergency created by a conspiracy which threatened the dissolution of the confederacy, a meeting of the Diet at Bern was ordered, and the cantons were notified to send deputies with special instructions for the foreshadowed crisis. Three measures were proposed; the formal expulsion of the Jesuits: the forcible dissolution of the Sonderbund, or a remodelled constitution whose articles should be in accord with the demands of the epoch.

Opposed to the seven Catholic cantons stood Zurich, Bern, Glarus, Schaffhausen, Grisons, Aargau, Thurgau, Ticino, Basel-Landschaft, and Outer-Appenzell. But as Basel-Landschaft was opposed by Basel-Stadt, and Outer-Appenzell by Appenzell-Intérieure, the votes of these two cantons were rendered nugatory. Geneva's deputy showed open partiality for the Sonderbund party, and even suggested the appointment of a committee to supervise the proceedings at Bern. In 1841, a political party, known as the "Third of March," had effected radical changes in the constitution of Geneva, and under their direction the management of cantonal affairs devolved upon a constituent council. At this epoch the decision of that body was favorable to the proposition of their deputy, and tremendous excitement resulted.

<small>The "Third of March."</small>

The liberal party declared null and void these decisions of their magistrates, the cantonal troops were repulsed by armed citizens; the ruling officers were speedily forced to resign their positions, and a new provisional government, under the leadership of James Fazy, was inaugurated, which elected a new deputy to the Diet, and gave the eleventh vote, in favor of armed dissolution of the Sonderbund.

Meanwhile, in the Reformed districts of the canton of Freyburg, a minority in opposition to the council, entered an urgent demand for withdrawal from the Sonderbund, and when this met refusal endeavored to effect their purpose by force. But their efforts were rendered fruitless by failure in discipline as well as by weakness in number, and Freyburg remained enrolled among the Sonderbund cantons.

In the elections of 1847 the canton of St. Gall arrived at a closely-contested point. Two parties in that district had for many years secured an equal constituency, and seventy-five radical deputies had opposed the same number of conservatives. But at this juncture the district of Gaster, hitherto conservative, chose liberal representatives, and the twelfth vote against the Sonderbund was secured.

# CHAPTER XXIII

## THE SONDERBUND WAR

### 1847

UNDER the pretence of threatened danger from members of the Free Corps, Luzern collected military stores, while all the Sonderbund cantons fortified their frontiers and prepared for a conflict. Encouraged by the sanction extended by the cabinets of Vienna and Paris, the League anticipated easy victory and the speedy establishment of Jesuit authority.

At this crisis the meeting of the Diet was a momentous event. Its proceedings were watched with breathless interest, and, during a few days of heated debate, anxiety throughout Switzerland grew intense. But on the 20th of July, from Bern, the *Vorort* of the confederacy, the decree went forth: "The Sonderbund must be dissolved!" and immediate imperative messages commanded all rebellious cantons to desist from offensive proceedings.

At the suggestion of Geneva's new deputy, the name of all staff-officers who refused immediate recognition of the authority of this decree were stricken from the roll of the confederacy, and the Diet then moved an adjournment to await the effect of its first mandate.

On the 3d of September the representatives reassembled at Bern for the purpose of discussing the postponed questions relating to the Jesuits, and by vote of a large majority decreed the expulsion of the order from Switzerland. The same Diet ordained a revision of the federal pact, and, before adjournment, appointed for the execution of that important commission a committee of fourteen distinguished members.

<small>Diet at Bern.</small>

The portent of tremendous events shadowed the land, and excitement was intense, although suppressed. The great council of Zurich, announcing its unalterable resolution to support the decisions of the Diet, exerted a widely disseminated influence. Quietly in the liberal cantons the councils assembled; quietly, but with firmness, their final decrees were uttered. In St. Gall, temporary disturbances were wrought by priestly interference, but liberal principles came forth triumphant, and the canton joined its loyal associates.

In Uri, Schwyz, and Unterwalden, tumultuous assemblies proclaimed a disposition to

## The Sonderbund War  273

support the Sonderbund League, and threatened loss of life or property to all who offered opposition.  In Valais and Freyburg, similar measures were pursued.  Zug wavered, but in Luzern only seven members of the council advised measures loyal to the Swiss Confederacy.  After a recess of eight weeks the Diet reassembled on the 18th of October.  The seven representatives of the Sonderbund cantons remained obstinately hostile, and refused either to dissolve their separate alliance, or to expel the Jesuits from their territory.  The loyal cantons opposed an open warfare, if any compromise consonant with the fundamental principles of the confederacy could be effected, and in a proclamation addressed to the rebellious cantons the Diet declared:—

"The rights and the freedom inherited from your fathers shall continue unaltered, your faith untouched.  The Diet desire no oppression of their confederate brothers, no nullifying of cantonal sovereignty, no forced change in the present confederate compact.  But the existence of a separate league, endangering the welfare of the whole, can never be allowed.  Dissolve it while yet there is time."

When this manifesto failed to elicit any response save that of resolute antagonism, and

**Civil War.**

mediation attempted by the cantons of Zug, Grisons, and Basel-Stadt proved fruitless, war was inevitable, and the Diet issued orders for the assembling of troops, over whom Henry Dufour of Geneva was appointed chief-in-command. By the Sonderbund this measure was characterized as a commencement of hostilities, and, casting upon the Diet the responsibility for all consequences, their deputies on the 29th of October quitted Bern. The remaining delegates to the assembly continued in session, and on the 4th of November publicly proclaimed a resolution to dissolve the Sonderbund by force of arms, while an army under excellent discipline hastened to complete its preparations for war. The Sonderbunders, whose aggressive measures had been pre-arranged, were enthusiastically eager for battle. Fanatical zeal among them had been stimulated by the influence of a papal nuncio, and Jesuit chaplains, who blessed their banners, distributed protective amulets, and promised to their cause the blessing of the Virgin. On the day of the Diet's proclamation of war, hostilities were opened by Sonderbund troops, one detachment passing over the St. Gothard into Ticino, while another band surprised an unprotected village in Aargau, and carried forty prisoners to Luzern.

NEAR KLOSTERS: SILBRETTA GLACIER.

Dufour made no haste to retaliate, although resolute in his determination utterly to subjugate the rebellious cantons. The controlling temper of the commander-in-chief was manifested in his charge to the assembled army. "I place under your protection children, women, old men, and the ministers of the Church. Come from this conflict victorious, but without stain."

An attack upon Freyburg was Dufour's first hostile exploit, and at that place an easy conquest was attained. The colonel of the Sonderbund troops, finding his city surrounded by the enemy, resigned his command, and the demoralized council gave immediate orders for the capitulation of the garrison. *Capture of Freyburg.*

This swift success secured the liberation of many prisoners, the termination of Jesuit influence in Freyburg, and the establishment of a liberal government in that city.

Meantime, a second division of the national army had directed its strength against Luzern and the forest cantons. Zug, thus threatened, hastily withdrew from the Sonderbund, and welcomed the loyal troops. At the Rothenburg and Meyers-Kappel the hostile armies met, and fought valiantly until victory rested with the confed- *Battles of the Rothenburg and Meyers-Kappel.*

erates. At Gislikon the advance of victorious divisions, under Egloff, Hausler, Einsberg, Benziger, and Moef, was fiercely disputed by the riflemen of Unterwalden, during a conflict enduring ten hours. The artillery of Solothurn was forced to retreat, but at that crisis a sudden and desperate charge of the Bernese compelled the Sonderbund troops to abandon their fortifications, and decided the contest. A general flight toward Luzern ensued, and on the following day the council of that city sent envoys to negotiate with Dufour, although, in a desperate hope of continuing the contest, some Sonderbund leaders fled over the lake to Altorf.

<small>Battle of Gislikon.</small>

Dufour insisted upon the unconditional surrender of Luzern, and after that event (November 25th) the submission of the minor cantons was inevitable. Unterwalden, Schwyz, and Uri soon capitulated, while the men prominent in the Sonderbund sought final asylum in Valais, there to await the promised intervention of France on their behalf. But Valais, their ultimate refuge, surrendered on the 28th of November; and at the end of twenty-five days the war was ended, the Sonderbund dissolved.

<small>Surrender of Luzern.</small>

## The Sonderbund War

In the cities of Freyburg and Luzern provisional governments restored the constitutions of 1830; Uri, for the first time since her heroic era, was provided with a written constitution. Extensive reforms were undertaken in Valais, Zug, and Unterwalden, and the Jesuits, pursued by an edict of perpetual banishment, fled precipitately from the country. Neuchâtel and Inner Appenzell, having refused to assist in the war, were compelled to pay a heavy fine to the confederacy, while the Sonderbund cantons were held responsible for debts contracted in consequence of their rebellion. The assessment for these debts could be secured only by armed occupation of the land, and, pressed by this contingency, the monks of St. Bernard, emigrated to Sardinia.

In the canton of Luzern many convents were suppressed, and their revenues employed for the benefit of the State, wherein serious financial embarrassment had been occasioned through the embezzlement of public funds by members of the old government.

At the conclusion of the war, while many prominent European nations were swift in sending congratulations to the Swiss Diet, Austria, standing aloof, offered asylum to the Jesuits and the exiled Sonderbunders, while

Rome loaded the victorious Swiss with reproaches, and the ambassador Montalembert, recalled to France, displayed there his eloquence in denunciations of the conquerors. It soon became evident that the purpose of the Swiss cantons to unite in a new and more intimate bond of federal union would encounter opposition from neighboring powers. Cabinets that had guaranteed the pact of 1815 claimed that the dissolution of that agreement was impossible without their formal consent, and messages of remonstrance or of menace were frequently received by the deputies assembled to frame the new constitution.

The Swiss Diet asserted its dignity in the brief response, "A free people must frame its own laws; we are vassals of no foreign power."

Soon after the termination of the Sonderbund war, the spirit of insurrection in France again rose to the surface; Louis Philippe was driven from his throne, and the swiftly-spreading impetus of the revolution caused neighboring governments to totter. But Switzerland maintained her equipoise upon the basis of federal freedom, although her borders were not unaffected by the storms without. The people of Neuchâtel, with a determination to free themselves from the compound rule of Prussian and cantonal officials, and to become wholly Swiss, summoned their state-council to abdicate. Upon the refusal of the magistrates to comply with this demand, a call to arms was sounded, a formidably enthusiastic company stormed the council-hall; in place of the Prussian eagle the white cross of the Swiss Confederation was erected, and all suggestions of compromise were vehemently rejected. Defensive operations, undertaken by troops of the government, showed so little zeal for the cause that the members of the council deemed it prudent to resign, with reservation of the royal rights. The republican army then secured possession of the city, and announced the termination of princely rule and the organization of a provisional government. Recognition was received from Bern, then *Vorort* of the Swiss Confederation, and to the remonstrances of the Prussian envoy, Von Sydow, the confederacy made reply:—

"Switzerland acknowledges no covenant with any prince of Neuchâtel. The canton entered our confederacy equal in rights to all others, and when she changes her government to suit herself we cannot oppose her."

Although thus supporting Neuchâtel, the Diet of 1849 refused the solicitations of Charles

Albert of Sardinia, to cement with him an offensive and defensive alliance against Austria. A few Swiss joined the army of Lombardy, but the majority of the nation declared their intention to remain neutral, although tempted to take part in the war by a widespread sympathy with the cause of Italian liberty. When fugitives, driven by Austrian victories into Grisons and Ticino, strove to kindle sparks of warfare in those districts, the Swiss government, guided by Ochsenbein and Munzinger, secured the admiration of its contemporaries by a dignified maintenance of neutrality throughout many perplexing complications.

# CHAPTER XXIV

## THE CONSTITUTIONS OF 1848 AND 1874

THE rampant spirit of war did not divert the Swiss Diet from the purpose of elaborating new articles of confederation, and April 8, 1848, a task was completed which gave to the cantons the first federal constitution compiled without foreign interference. The political divisions recognized were those of the twenty-two cantons named in the pact of 1815; and while each of these was endowed with a wide liberty within its own borders, the new pact united all by a stronger central tie than any previous terms of confederation had forged.

Modelled in some measure upon the constitution of the United States of America, the new central government was vested in a Federal Assembly, to which individual cantons yielded a portion of the authority they had hitherto claimed. This Federal Assembly was divided into two legislative chambers, — the National Council (*National*

*The Central Government.*

*Rath*) and the Council of States (*Stände Rath*), To the first of these, every Swiss over twenty-one years of age was eligible, the successful **The National Council.** candidate entering office through an election by ballot, for a term of three years. Each canton was entitled to elect one deputy for every twenty thousand of population.

The Council of States consisted of two deputies **The Council of States.** from each canton, who were nominated by the magistrates of their states.

The Federal Assembly nominated the seven members of a Federal Council or Executive (*Bundesrath*), which was separated into departments, and presided over by the President of the Confederation.

The chief officer of the confederacy was to be chosen from the members of the Federal Council, and was subject to an annual election. Bern, on account of its position between the French and German speaking districts, was chosen as the seat of the central government. Liberty of the press was established, all denominations of Christians within the community were guaranteed freedom of worship; but the Jesuits, with allied religious orders, were excluded from the land. German, French, and

Italian were recognized as national languages, and were severally used in the published proclamations of the Assembly's decrees, and in the announcement of their votes; but Italian members of the Executive were supposed to understand either French or German, and speeches were to be translated into those tongues only.

*Languages.*

On the 17th of June, 1848, the new constitution was completed. It was promptly accepted by thirteen and a half cantons, and with little delay by all except Schwyz, Uri, and Zug. During the summer the sanction of these states was also rendered, and on the 12th of September, with pealing of bells and blazing of mountain fires, the most perfect union in Swiss annals was inaugurated.

Upon a few points, where cantonal or federal authority had failed of satisfactory readjustment, subsequent legislation slightly modified the constitution of 1848; but for a considerable period affairs of internal interest absorbed the public attention, and important results were exhibited in an improved monetary system, and a uniform scale of weights and measures (1851).

In 1852 the King of Prussia declared his intention to resume authority in Neuchâtel;

but three thousand royalists, who gathered at Vilangen to support his cause, found their schemes frustrated by the union of seven thousand republicans. In 1856, a conspiracy, formed by the royalists, to arrest the state-council at Neuchâtel, was successfully carried into execution, but the deed met swift revenge, and over six hundred prisoners were secured by the republicans, who, retaining but twenty-eight ringleaders for trial as insurgents, allowed the remainder to return to their homes. Frederick William IV. of Prussia demanded the release of the prisoners, and upon the refusal to grant this behest, threatened war; but French mediation was proffered, and Louis Napoleon promised freedom to the captives. The Federal government refused to permit their liberation, **Freedom of Neuchâtel.** without a guarantee of the freedom of Neuchâtel, and upon this point the dispute waxed so bitter, that in 1857 thirty thousand men were stationed along the Swiss frontier, under command of the veteran Dufour.

Napoleon's tactics then became more conciliatory, the Federal government accepted his intervention, the prisoners were released, and a treaty was signed at Paris by which the King of Prussia, though retaining the title of "Prince

THE AXENSTRASSE.

of Neuchâtel," renounced all claim to rule over the territory.

During the period of the Austro-Italian wars, the neutrality of its southern frontier was jealously guarded by the Swiss government, and serious entanglements were thus avoided, although some embarrassing complications occurred. The city of Perouse, refusing to receive a papal garrison, was taken by Swiss soldiers serving in the papal army. The Federal Council, in order utterly to repudiate responsibility for this and similar entanglements, decreed that Swiss regiments serving in Italy should not carry their national ensign. The promulgation of this ordinance in Naples, provoked insubordination among the Swiss troops, which increased, until, by command of the King, their regiments were disbanded. Although some soldiers enrolled themselves under new commanders, many returned home, where the enactment of rigorous laws, greatly restricted, thenceforth, the foreign military service.

In 1860, France, long covetous of Savoy, secured from Victor Emmanuel the cession of that district and of Nice, sacrificing thereby the favor of the Swiss; but in 1862 the restitution to Vaud of the valley of Dappes, which had been seized by Napoleon I., proved a conciliatory measure, and in 1864 a commercial treaty of signal advantage to Switzerland was consummated with the French nation.

In Geneva a new era of prosperity was inaugurated under the liberal government of Fazy. The city was extended by the removal of old ramparts, and the Roman Catholics were granted protection in the exercise of their faith. Varying political interests provoked animosities during the election period of 1864, and strife in the city forced the Federal government to a military occupation of the canton and the arrest of leaders from antagonistic factions. But in 1869, in peace and harmony, the city made glad holiday, and, by the erection of a noble statue on the border of the lake, celebrated the anniversary of its union with the Swiss Confederacy.

*Fazy in Geneva.*

At a convention held in Geneva in 1864, deputies from the chief nations of Europe chose Switzerland to be the centre of various international unions subsequently consummated. The establishment at Bern, in 1865, of the International Telegraph Office was swiftly followed by that of the Postal Union, and other partnerships for the protection and promotion of industrial, literary, and artistic enterprises.

At the breaking out of the Franco-Prussian

war (1870), the Federal Council, anticipating violation of Switzerland's neutrality, by armies of the antagonistic nations, ordered out troops for frontier duty. The aged Dufour was again chosen chief-in-command, but at eighty-five years of age declined the responsibility, which was then intrusted to Hans Herzog of Aargau. Under his direction, faithful surveillance along the Swiss boundaries was continued, until the line of conflict had shifted to the north and west, and danger to Switzerland seemed averted. In January, 1871, a report that Bourbaki would attempt to enter Germany by the Rhine caused the disbanded troops to be again assembled for the protection of the bridge at Basle; but soon afterwards a Prussian victory threatened the capture of the entire force under the French commander, unless in this extremity asylum upon Swiss territory could be secured. Rumors of Bourbaki's intention to force an entrance elicited from Herzog a published protest, but the hospitality sought was subsequently granted upon condition of a surrender of arms at the frontier. Officers in command of the fugitives were prompt in their acceptance of these stipulations, and eighty-three thousand French troops were quietly disarmed and sheltered.

In 1872, with the ultimate object of extending the prerogatives of the central government, an amendment to the Constitution was proposed. The proposition, then rejected, met favorable reception by a large majority two years later, when, "to give the people a more direct share in legislation," the privileges of "the Initiative" and "the Referendum" were established. The first franchise secures the submission to popular vote of any petition endorsed by a certain number of qualified persons, the requisite number of signatures for cantonal affairs being five thousand, and for federal matters fifty thousand. The Referendum secures the reference of all laws, passed in cantonal or in federal assemblies, to as large a body of voters as can be convened.

*Constitutional Amendments.*

*The Initiative.*

*The Referendum.*

The Federal Tribunal, a court of justice for the cantons with enlarged jurisdiction, was soon afterward established at Lausanne, where, in 1886, the new "Palace of Justice" opened its municipal doors.

Universal provision for free elementary education was assured, and cantonal rights were everywhere guaranteed after a three-years' residence.

## Constitutions of 1848 and 1874

The Constitution thus amended, and accepted by fourteen and one-half cantons (1874), still remains in force. Individual cantons are authorized to treat with foreign powers only through the medium of the federal government, but the exercise of this central authority is maintained in entire harmony with cantonal rights, and each canton preserves the privilege of choosing its form of internal rule. Uri, Glarus, the Unterwalden, and Appenzell districts continue their ancient *Landesgemeinden*, and annually, in May, the peasants assemble in holiday garb, to meet their *Landammann*, who, at the conclusion of a religious service, recites to his "trusty, faithful, and well-beloved countrymen," the worthy deeds of their ancestors, and bids them, thus counselled by example, decide the course of their future story.

In some cantons, representative bodies take the place of popular assemblies; but the forms of legislation are as varied as republican principles permit. Bern, Thurgau, and a few other divisions, reserve the right to veto laws passed in their district assemblies. In Zurich any two harmonious citizens can present a new law for popular consideration.

The division of cantons into communes dates

back, according to an eminent authority,[1] to the period of the abolition of the feudal system, when the enfranchisement of the people called into existence many small communities who claimed prerogatives in accordance with the freedom of their canton, but remained subservient to the enactments of their representatives. A commune answers to an English county.

*Communes.*

It has been said that in Switzerland the "first business of the State is keeping school." Education is compulsory and gratuitous in all primary grades, and the provision for public instruction and for the construction and preservation of roads form the most important items of public expenditure. The system of Pestalozzi of Zurich (born 1746), the founder of a school at Yverdon, forms the basis of the educational methods pursued, and in all villages communal authority nominates the schoolmaster, and superintends the school. Scattered throughout Switzerland are six thousand primary schools, and attendance, at least once a week, for six years, is enforced, although, in the season of harvesting, a half-day's attendance is remitted. In 1877

*System of Public Instruction.*

---

[1] See Adams and Cunningham on "The Swiss Confederation."

## Constitutions of 1848 and 1874

a law forbade the employment in mill or in workshop of children under fifteen years.

By cantonal law the lowest salary of the schoolmaster is fixed at three hundred and fifty francs per annum, and the punishment of a fine is decreed to any one accepting a smaller sum for the services of this office.

In fourteen cantons, and in portions of others, German is the spoken language; French is the common tongue in three and in portions of three others; while Italian is confined to Ticino, and a part of Grisons.

German names have been retained in the first seventeen cantons, except in Graubünden, where "Grisons" is commonly used; the eighteenth canton keeps its Italian name, "Ticino," while the remainder bear French cognomens, with the modification of Geneva for "Genève." *Cantonal Names.*

In September, 1890, a widespread excitement was induced by an uprising in the canton of Ticino, where, since 1873, a conservative government had been in power. *Uprising in Ticino.* Prompted by the discovery of dishonest practices at elections, ten thousand radicals signed a petition for a revision of their constitution; but instead of submitting the proposal to a popular vote, as both law and custom demanded, the authorities delayed action, on pretence of verifying the signatures appended to the document. Impatient of the delay, the radicals appealed to the Federal Council, and, failing to receive immediate response from that body, summarily seized and imprisoned three members of the cantonal council, while another, named Rossi, who attempted resistance, was killed, and several prominent men fled from the country. A provisional government organized by the insurgents was supported by an excited populace, who seized the telegraph offices, and defied the authorities. But the appearance of a federal commissioner, supported by a military force, sufficed to quell the storm, and to this authority the canton was temporarily subjected. On the 5th of October a popular vote in favor of a revision of the constitution was supported by the Federal Council, and in a trial held at Zurich, the leaders of the insurrection were freely acquitted, with the single exception of Castione, the murderer of Rossi.

The sympathy of the civilized world was extended to Switzerland in 1892 when a landslide at St. Gervais-les-Bains in Savoy buried houses with their inhabitants, and, shaking the support of glaciers, swept seas of ice down the mountain-sides that crushed or drowned multitudes, and completely demolished the village of Le Fayet.

. . . . . . . .

By the constitutions of 1848 and 1874 the Swiss Confederation ceased to be "a union without unity," and became a unified nation in which the twenty-two cantons are vital political divisions. Bound together by principles preserved through a long fellowship of conflict and of endurance, Switzerland, "an Alpine battery against oppression," has also been surnamed "The Land of Unfulfilled Destiny."

# INDEX

AARAU, peace of, 224.
Aargau, Hapsburg nobility in, 38; capture of, 68; religious conflicts in, 261.
Adolf of Nassau, 26.
Agnadello, battle of, 129.
Aix, battle of, 7.
Aix-la-Chapelle, peace of, 228.
Albert of Austria, 24, 26; assassination of, 31.
Alliance, the "Perpetual," 25; the French, 124; the Holy, 254.
Alpinus, Julius, 11.
Alsace, 79, 81, 84, 90.
Altorf, village of, 28.
Amadeus VIII., Duke, 72.
Am Buel, Matthias, 56.
Amendments, constitutional, 288.
Amiens, treaty of, 244.
Ammann, the, 19.
Amstein, John, 57.
Anabaptists, the, 140; fanaticism of the, 145.
Apostle of Switzerland, the, 133.
Appenzell, 58, 59, 63; admission of, 120; the men of, 60.
Arbeddo, battle of, 72.
Armagnacs, the, 77.
Arnold of Brescia, 131.
Arnold of Cervola, 49.
Arnold of Melchthal, 27, 28.
Associate-districts, 113.

Austria, Albert of, 24, 26, 31; Frederick of, 33; Leopold of, 33, 55; Leopold III. of, 49; Leopold IV. of, 58, 60, 62.
Austria, truce with, 79.
Austrian Alliance, 76.
Aux, Isbrand d', 206.

BADEN, conference at, 146, 147; siege of, 77.
Bailiffs, imperial, 26.
Bailiwicks, free, 70.
Baillod, Jacques, 189.
Balderon, 211, 212.
Balm, Rudolf of, 31.
Basle, 49; council of, 67; peace of, 119; admission of, 119.
Baume, Pierre del a, 162, 166, 168, 169, 171, 172, 174, 183, 184, 185, 187.
Bavaria, Louis of, 33.
Bayard, the Chevalier, 126.
Beauharnais, Hortense, 256.
Bellegarde, the Sire de, 175.
Benziger, 276.
Berengen of Landenberg, 26.
Bern, 42, 44, 50, 52, 57, 58, 62, 68, 72; meeting at, 76; disturbances in, 229; Diet at, 272, 273, 274.
Berthelier, 156, 157, 158, 160, 161.
Berthier, 247.
Bohemia, Ottacar of, 24.

# Index

Bonnivard, Francis, 157, 160, 174, 175, 176, 190.
Borromean League, the, 205, 206.
Borromeo, Cardinal Charles, 205.
Bourbaki, 287.
Brandenburg peace, the, 46, 53.
Brun, Rudolf, 40.
Brune, General, 239, 240.
Brunnen, Bund of, 35.
Bubenberg, Adrian von, 103, 108.
Bull, the Golden, 171.
Bullinger, Henry, 150.
Bundesbrief, the Latin, 25.
Burgundy, kingdom of, 14; Philip of, 77; Mary of, 99; Charles the Bold of, 80, 85, 86, 107, 111.
Büttisholtz, battle of, 50.

CALIXTINES, the, 67
Calvin, 192, 193, 195, 196; marriage of, 198; letter to Sadoleto, 197; character of, 200; death of, 203.
Cambray, league of, 126, 127.
Campobasso, 110.
Canal, the Linth, 247.
Cassius, Lucius, 7.
Castione, 292.
Cecina, Aulus, 11.
Cervola, Arnold of, 49.
Charlemagne, 16.
Charles the Bold, 80, 85, 86, 107, 111.
Charles IV. of Germany, 46.
Charles V. of Germany, 138.
Charles Albert of Sardinia, 279.
Charter, the Women's, 58.
Chenaux, Nicholas, 230, 231.
Chillon, capture of, 190.
Christianity, introduction of, 14.
Chur, Bishop of, 21.
Cimbri, the, 6.
Cisalpine Republic, the, 238.
Cities, growth of, 17.
Clovis, divisions under, 14.
Colonna, Prosper, 129.

Communes, the, 290.
Compactata, the, 67.
Condottieri, the, 49.
Congress of Vienna, the, 249.
Conseil, 255.
Constance, Council of, 65, 66, 68; peace of, 79; Diet of, 126.
Constitution of Switzerland, 281, 289.
Controversies, religious, 138.
Council of Horn, the, 117.
Council of States, the, 282.
Courcy, Ingram de, 49, 50.

DAY of the Ladders, the, 173.
Deinikon, peace of, 150.
Dominican brotherhood, the, 132.
Diebold of Basilwind, 43.
Diesbach, 83, 91, 93, 108.
Diet of Constance, the, 126.
Diet of Stanz, the, 114.
Diet of 1522, the, 141.
Diet, of Zurich the, 120.
Diet, the Swiss, 278.
Diviko, 7, 9.
Dornach, battle of, 119.
Dornbuhl, battle of the, 42.
Dufour, Henry, 274, 275, 276, 287.
Duomo d'Ossola, 70.
Duval, General, 224.

EGLOFF, 276.
Eidgenossen, the, 159.
Einsberg, 276.
Einsiedeln, abbey of, 15; abbot of, 20, 33; assembly at, 141.
Embassy to France, 108.
Emmenegger, 217, 220.
Empire, freedom from the, 119.
Entlibuch, 50.
Erlach, General, 219.
Erlach, Rudolf von, 43, 44, 94.
Escalade, the, 207, 208.
Eschenbach, Walter of, 32.
Estavayer, the "Bad Day" of, 92.
Evangelicals, the, 162.

## Index

Evangelists in Geneva, the, 181.
Everhard, 45.

FAREL, William, 180, 181, 182, 186, 188, 189, 192, 193, 194, 196.
Fazy, James, 269; government of, 286.
Federal Assembly, the, 281, 282; Federal Council, the, 282, 287.
Feldkirch, covenant of, 84; treaty of, 213.
Felix and Regula, 39.
Felix V., Pope, 156.
Flagellants, the, 47.
Foix, Gaston de, 127.
Foreign governments, complications with, 255.
France, treaty with, 78; interference of, 190.
Francis I. of France, 129, 138, 190.
Franciscan Brotherhood, the, 132.
Franco-Prussian War, the, 287.
Frastanz, battle of, 118.
Frauenbrief, the, 58
Frederick II. of Germany, 23.
Frederick V. of Germany, 76, 86.
Frederick of the Empty Pocket, 62, 63, 68.
Frederick of Austria, 33.
Freyburg, 62; Diet at, 108; insurrection in, 230; capture of, 275.
Froment, 181, 189.
Fuctor, 229.
Furbity, 186.
Fürst, Walther, 28

GENEVA, 94, 161, 162, 231; fairs in, 93; early government of, 153, 154; aid for, 159; laws of, 194, 195, 199; alliance between the Swiss and, 168; schools of, 200; constitutional changes in, 233, 235; united to France, 236; convention in, 286.

Gesler, Hermann, 26, 27, 28, 29.
Giants, battle of the, 129.
Gingens, battle of, 189.
Giornico, battle of, 113.
Gislikon, battle of, 276.
Glarus, 46, 56, 57, 60, 68.
God's-House League, the, 74, 75.
Government, the Helvetic, 243; the Central, of Switzerland, 281.
Grandson, siege of, 98; battle of, 100; surrender of, 99.
Grisons, 75; civil war in, 209; the St. Bartholomew of the, 210; freedom of, 213.
Gundoldingen, 55.
Gypsies, 73.

HAGENBACH, 81, 85.
Halberds, Council of, 165.
Halwyl, John of, 106.
Hapsburg, Counts of, 21; Albert III. of, 21; Rudolf I. of, 22; Rudolf II. of, 22, 23; Rudolf III. of, 23, 24, 37.
Hassfurter, 108.
Hausler, 276.
Helvetians, the, 6, 8, 9, 11, 12, 16, 19.
Henry of Luxemburg, 32, 33.
Henzi, Samuel, 229.
Hericault, fortress of, 87.
Herterstein, 108.
Herzog, Hans, 287.
Herzogenbuchsee, battle of, 219.
Hess, Burgomaster, 260.
Hesse, Landgrave of, 148, 152.
Hildegarde, the Abbess, 39.
Hochberg, Rudolf of, 95.
Hofen, Thomas ab, 170.
Hordrich, 8.
Hugues, Besançon, 159, 164, 168.
Huguenots, the, 159, 166, 180, 182.
Huss, John, 65, 66, 131.
Hussites, the, 67.
Huzel, Bernard, 260.

## 298 Index

INNOCENT IV., Pope, 23.
Initiative, the, 288.
"Institutes," Calvin's, 193.
Instruction, system of public, 290.
Italian territory, 112.

JEALOUSIES, cantonal, 114.
Jenatsch, 211, 212.
Jerome of Prague, 67, 131.
Jesuits, the, 265, 272.
Jetzer, 132, 133.
John of Trocznow, 67.
Julius II., Pope, 127, 128.

KAPPEL, battle of, 149.
Kätzy, Ulric, 105, 108.
Keller, Augustine, 261.
Kuno of Staufen, 59, 60.
Küssnacht, castle of, 29.
Kyburg, Counts of, 21, 52.

LA HARPE, Francis Cæsar, 238.
Lake dwellers, the, 5.
"La Mazze," 71.
Landammann, 45, 246.
Landenberg, 26, 27, 31.
Landesgemeinden, 45, 246.
Languages of Switzerland, the, 13, 283, 291.
Laupen, town of, 43, 44.
Lausanne, 94, 97.
League, the Gray, 74.
League, the God's-House, 74, 75.
League of the Ten Jurisdictions, the, 74.
League of Three Lands, the, 23.
League of St. George, the, 62.
League of St. Omer, 81, 82.
League, the Holy, 127.
League of Cambray, 126, 127.
League, the Borromean, 205, 206.
League, the Spoon, 171, 176.
League of Rothen, 263.
Leipsic, battle of, 248.
Lemanic republic, the, 239.
Leo X., Pope, 136, 137.

Leodegar, the Abbot, 222, 223, 225.
Leopold of Austria, 33, 35.
Leopold III. of Austria, 49.
Leopold IV. of Austria, 58, 60, 62.
Leu, Joseph, 262, 263.
Levantina, the, 72.
Levrier, Aimé, 163.
Libertines, the, 195, 202.
Longueville, Henri de, 215.
Louis XI. of France, 90.
Louis XII. of France, 126, 128.
Louis of Bavaria, 33.
Louis Philippe, 278.
Luther, doctrines of, 151, 152.
Luxemburg, Henry of, 32, 33.
Luzern, 7, 18, 37, 38, 46, 53, 58, 68, 71, 72; Council at, 75; insurrection in, 262.

MAISONNEUVE, Baudichon de la, 186, 187.
Mamelukes, the, 160, 163, 182.
Marburg, disputation at, 152.
Marignano, battle of, 129.
Massena, 243.
Massner, Thomas, 227, 228.
Maximilian of Austria, 99.
Maximilian the Emperor, 117, 125.
Mediation, the Act of, 245, 249, 257.
Meinrod, 15.
Mercenary service, 110.
Meyers-Kappel, battle of, 275.
Micheli of Crest, 232.
Milan, the Duke of, 70, 73, 91; treaty of, 213.
Milch-Suppe, the, 149.
Moef, 276.
Montalembert, 276.
Montebello, the Duke of, 255.
Morat, 92, 103; siege of, 104; battle of, 106.
Morgarten, battle of, 34.
Morgarten of Appenzell, the, 60.
Münster, battle of, 72.
Murbach abbey, 37.
Muri, abbey of, 258.

# Index 299

Näfels, battle of, 56.
Names, cantonal, 291.
Nancy, battle of, 110.
Napoleon, 238, 244, 245, 247, 248.
Napoleon, Louis, 256, 257.
National Council, the, 282.
Navarre, Henry of, 207.
Neuchâtel, 247, 250, 254, 279, 280, 284; Henri de, 87; Margrave of, 95.
Nicholas of the Flue, 115.
Novara, battle of, 128.
Noviodunum, 9.
Nyon, 9.

Oberwalden, the hermit of, 115.
Oberwangen, battle of, 42.
Ochsenbein, Ulrich, 266.
Old Switzerland, the party of, 264.
Olivetan, Peter Robert, 180.
Orbe, 89.
Orgetorix, 8.
Ottacar of Bohemia, 24.

Pact, the Federal, 250, 258; the Rossi, 253.
Peace, the "Bad," 55; the "Rotten," 77; of Constance, 78; the Perpetual, 130.
Peasants' Revolt, the, 216, 217, 218, 219.
Perpetual Alliance, the, 25.
Pestalozzi, 290.
Pfaffenbrief, the, 48.
Pfyffer, Colonel, 221.
Pfyffer, Louis, 206.
Pisa, Council of, 64.
Plague, the great, 47.
Planta, Pompey, 209, 210.
Pleurs, landslide at, 208.
Pontverre, the Sire de, 172.
Progress, intellectual, 122.

Rapperswyl, counts of, 21; John of, 40; siege of, 77.
Raron, the Baron of, 70, 71, 72.

Rastadt, Congress of, 239.
Ratisbon, Peace of, 46.
Reding, Rudolf, 34.
Reding, Itel, 75, 78, 108.
Reding, Aloys, 241.
Referendum, the, 288.
Reformed Religion, establishment of the, in Geneva, 191.
Regula and Felix, 39.
Reichenbach, castle of, 44.
Religious war, first, 221; second, 222.
Religious divisions, 257.
René of Lorraine, 105, 109.
Renée, the Duchess, 193.
Republic, the Helvetic, 241, 257.
"Restraint," Uri's, 27, 31.
Rhetia, 5, 74, 75.
Rhetians, the, 5, 10, 13.
Rhetus, 5.
Riedi, Thomas, 72.
Romans, contact with the, 7; sway of the, 10.
Romont, Count of, 91.
Rossi, 292.
Rosenthurm, battle of, 241.
Rothen, the League of, 263.
Rothenburg, Count of, 53; battle of the, 275.
Rott, John, 52.
Rotzberg, castle of, 31.
Rousseau, Jean Jacques, 233.
Rudolf of Kyburg, 51.
Rudolf of Erlach, 43.
Rütli, meadow of, 28; men of, 30; oath of, 31.

Sadoleto, letter of, 197.
Sales, Francis de, 205.
Salis, 209.
Sampson, Bernard, 136.
Sarnenbund, the, 253.
Saunier, 180.
Savoy, 94; conflicts with, 70; Peter of, 155; Amadeus VIII. of, 155; John of, 157, 162;

Charles III. of, 157, 158, 162, 163, 176, 177, 178, 191; treachery of, 158; Emanuel Philibert of, 191, 204, 206; Charles Emanuel of, 207.
Schaffhausen, 18; admission of, 120.
Schinner, Matthew, 127.
Schwarzwald, the, 79.
Schwyz, 6, 7, 22, 23, 25, 26, 32, 44, 46, 60, 75; freemen of, 19; men of, 34.
Säckingen, the abbess of, 21.
Sempach, battle of, 53.
Sentis, the, 59.
Servetus, 201, 202.
Service, mercenary, 123.
Sforza, Galeas, 88.
Sforza, Ludovico, 125.
Sforza, Maximilian, 128, 129.
Siebnerbund, the, 254.
Sigismund of Germany, 66, 67, 68, 79, 84.
Silenen, Jost von, 95.
Silenen, Albert von, 108.
Simplon, the, 247.
Socinius, 204.
Solothurn, 51, 52, 57, 63.
Sonderbund, the, 267, 268, 269, 270, 271, 273, 276, 277.
Sonnenberg, General, 267.
Speicher, defile of, 60.
Spurs, battle of the, 128.
Staeffa, 238.
Stanz, Diet of, 114; covenant of, 115.
States, Confederation of Thirteen, 120.
Stauffacher, Werner, 27, 28.
Steiger, Frederick, 239.
Steiger, Paul, 243.
Steiger, Dr., 266.
St. Gall, 15, 16; Abbot of, 21, 59, 62, 79, 243.
St. Gervais-les-Bains, landslide at, 292.

St. Gothard, 70.
St. Jacob, chapel of, 35.
St. Jacob on the Birs, battle of, 78.
St. Jacob on the Sihl, battle of, 77.
St. Julien, peace of, 208; truce of, 178.
Stoss, battle of the, 61.
Strauss, Frederick, 259.
Stüssi, 75, 76, 77.
St. Victor's, priory of, 157, 174, 175; destruction of, 188.
Swabia, John of, 31.
Swabian wars, the, 118.
Switer and Swen, 5.
Switzerland, name first used, 246.

TABORITES, the, 67.
Tell, William, 28, 29.
"Terrier," the, 31, 32.
Teutones, the, 6.
Theilig of Luzern, 116.
Thiers, M. 255.
"Third of March," the, 269.
Thirty Years' War, the, 214.
Thorberg, Peter of, 53.
Thurgau, 6, 79.
Ticino, uprising in, 291.
Toggenburg, Counts of, 74, 75; district of, 79; question, the, 222, 223.
Trembly, 233.
Tribunal, the federal, 288.
Trient, battle at the, 265.
Tuileries guard, massacre of the, 237.
Turmann, Rudolf, 125.

ULRICHEN, battle of, 72.
Unterwalden, 7, 22, 23, 25, 33, 44, 46, 50, 60, 71; the horns of, 100; riflemen of, 276.
Uri, 7, 22, 23, 25, 26, 32, 44, 68; 70, 71; charter of, 22; the horns of, 100.
Utraquists, the, 67.

# Index

VALAIS, 71, 91; disturbances in, 263, 264.
Val d'Ossola, the, 72.
Valtelina, the, 209, 210, 212, 238.
Vauxmarcus, castle of, 99.
Vendôme, the Duc de, 227.
Vercellæ, battle of, 7.
Vervins, treaty of, 207.
Victor Emmanuel, 285.
Villmergen, battle of, 221, 261; second battle of, 224.
Viret, 180, 186, 189, 196.
Vögelinsegg, battle on the, 60.
Vorort, the, 44, 120, 246.

WALDMANN, 108; Hans, 116; convention of, 117.
Waldshut, siege of, 79; treaty of, 80.
Waldstätten, the, 26, 36, 41, 42, 44, 48, 49, 50, 68, 70.
Waterloo, battle of, 249.
Wattenwyl, Jean de, 207.
Wenceslaus, King, 67.
Werdenberg, Rudolf of, 61, 62.
Werner, 229.
Wernli, Pierre, 183.

Wesen, town of, 56.
Westphalia, peace of, 215.
Wettstein, Rudolf, 215.
Wildermuth, 189.
Winkelried, Arnold von, 54.
Winterthur, 35.
Wurtemberg, Count of, 45.

YOLANDE of Savoy, 88, 91.
Young Switzerland, party of, 264.
Yverdon, 96.

ZERINGEN, thirty lords of, 19; Berchthold V. of, 42.
Ziska, 67.
Zug, 46, 48, 57, 68.
Zurich, 16, 38, 39, 41, 44, 48, 50, 57, 58, 68, 75, 137; the Reformation in, 139, 140; troops of, 78.
Zurich and Austria, alliance between, 76.
Zurich, insurrection in, 116.
Zwingli Ulrich, 133, 134; call to Zurich, 135; in Zurich, 136, 137, 138, 139, 142, 143, 144; theology of, 145, 151, 152; death of, 149.

www.ingramcontent.com/pod-product-compliance
Lightning Source LLC
Chambersburg PA
CBHW031426230426
43668CB00007B/457